THE LIGHTNING CAMPAIGN

The Lightning Campaign
The Indo-Pakistan War, 1971

Major General D.K. PALIT, VrC (Retd)

LANCER PUBLISHERS ■ **SPANTECH & LANCER**

New Delhi • London • Hartford Wi

Published in India by
Lancer Publishers & Distributors
56 Gautam Nagar, New Delhi 110 049,
in the United Kingdom by
Spantech & Lancer,
Lagham Road, South Godstone,
Surrey RH9 8HB England,
and in the United States by
Spantech & Lancer
3986 Ernst Road, Hartford, Wi 53027

Published in arrangement with
Thomson Press
First published in 1972

© 1998, Major General D.K. Palit

Printed at Tarun Offset, Delhi

ISBN 1 897829 37 X

British Library Cataloguing-in-Publication Data.
A catalogue record for this book is available
from the British Library

*This book is dedicated to all those who
fought for the liberation of Bangla Desh*

THE INDIAN ARMED FORCES
THE BORDER SECURITY FORCE
THE CENTRAL ARMED POLICE
THE MUKTI BAHINI

and
The people of Bangla Desh

Contents

Maps and Sketches

Preface

When the Publishers first approached me to write a book on the war and to complete the manuscript within 15 days, there was some hesitation on my part—not because the task could not be completed within the stipulated period but because a war history written so soon after the event might not succeed in presenting the narrative with objectivity. In any case, the war was not officially over—only a ceasefire had been agreed upon. The western front was still on the alert; given the fanaticism and chaos that gripped Pakistanis after they were informed of the total defeat of their much vaunted soldiery in Bangla Desh, it was not unlikely that they might unleash some form of suicidal and frenzied *jehad*. In these circumstances there could be no lifting of security regarding information from Western and Southern Command.

At the same time, there were many in India eagerly awaiting an early and comprehensive account of the war, which they sensed was somehow different from India's other wars—not only because it was apparent, even to the layman, that this time there had been a different kind of technique: but also that it had been planned and directed with professional precision, executed with consummate skill. Government machinery handling the publicity had been better organised, more forthcoming and credible—and this had brought the war closer to the man-in-the-street. Finally, the unexpectedly early defeat of what had been reckoned to be a formidable enemy excited widespread interest in the military conduct of the campaign. All these factors contributed towards a growing demand for an early book on the Bangla Desh campaign.

The difficulty about writing a book so soon after the event is that lack of documentation and authentication prevents the author from recording details of operations, moves and identification of formations and units. However, what was required at this stage was an overall analysis of the major events and objective commentary: students of the campaign requiring greater details will have to wait for the official history—which might take months, or even years, in compilation.

I have not used any matter that could be classified as security but compiled my account mainly from discussions with former colleagues and friends who were in a position to give me authoritative opinions; from press reports—both Indian and foreign —and, above all, from my own knowledge and experience.

There was a trace of personal commitment in the writing of this narrative—if only because of the personalities involved. "Jaggi" Aurora, then a Gentleman-Cadet Corporal, was my section commander at the Indian Military Academy in 1938, when Yahya Khan was a Gentleman-Cadet Lance Corporal, one term "Jaggi's" junior. Niazi came later—I am not sure if he had even entered the Academy before "Jaggi" and Yahya were commissioned. Yahya and I served in the same Regiment—Baluch—as did Yahya's Chief of Staff, Hamid Khan, though we never met again after the Second World War started. "Jaggi" Aurora and I served together some twenty years later as Divisional Commanders in the same Corps (and, incidentally, the one that struck at Dacca from "Jaggi's" eastern theatre). I wish I had thought of asking for his autograph then.

The three Corps Commanders in Eastern Command were also close friends—Mohan Thapan and I were at the Academy at the same time, though he was a year senior; Sagat Singh and I were Colonels of Regiment of sister regiments of Gorkhas; "Tappy" Raina and I served together in Military Secretary's Branch at Army Headquarters. Little wonder that as the campaign in Bangla Desh progressed, I awaited news from the various sectors with more than just an historian's eagerness.

I record my debt to the willing cooperation extended to

me by the Press Information Bureau of the Government of India and for giving me permission to use their maps and photographs.

I acknowledge with gratitude the generous support given me by Mr K. Subrahmanyam of the Institute of Defence Studies and Analyses, not only for placing the resources of his organisation at my disposal but also for his personal interest and advice. My publishers, Messrs Thomson Group of New Delhi, placed their secretarial services at my disposal and helped in a number of other engagingly informal ways— and I record my debt to them also.

Lastly, my very special thanks are due to my research assistant, Pamela Burdick, without whose help I could not have hoped to meet the deadline set by the publishers. Although inhibited by her diplomatic status from taking any part in the drafting, she never hesitated to meet my urgent demands on the numerous mechanical tasks of a research and secretarial nature that the preparation of a book such as this entailed.

(D.K. PALIT)
Major-General (Retd)

Palisade, Dehra Dun
January 14, 1972

Introduction

Few campaigns in history have caused as much surprise and speculation as the Indian Armed Forces' liberation of Bangla Desh: and with good reason.

During twenty-four years as an independent entity, the Indian Army has been almost continuously engaged in operations: Hyderabad; the Kashmir war of 1947–48 and the permanent state of confrontation that was its heritage; operations in Nagaland; the Chinese confrontation and the consequent war of 1962 (in which its performance was so poor); the Mizo Hills insurgency; and the undeclared war with Pakistan in 1965. The Air Force was involved in some of these wars in a combat role, in others only in transport operations, though always crucially. The Navy stood in the wings, never having been given the chance to come into its own.

From all these conflicts, the watching world formed an image of our military machine: the verdict—a good second-class British left-over, steadily declining in operational potential. Surprisingly self-sufficient in weapons and ammunition for a developing nation—it was nevertheless on the wane in actual combat capability. At best it could be considered comparable to the Pakistani armed forces—but, certainly in Western eyes, even that was debatable.

Suddenly, it seems to have pulled a rabbit out of the hat. After a period of seeming impotence during the earlier part of the Bangla Desh crisis, which was perhaps the most critical period of our history, the Indian armed forces executed, within the brief period of 12 days, the most decisive liberation campaign in military history—giving a nation of 75 million people its independence in one lightning strike. Operating in one of the most difficult terrains in the world—in which the few existing national highways and railway systems had been disrupted by their insurgent allies—Indian forces, moving with incredible swiftness, brought a formidable enemy to his knees and took 93,000 of them prisoner. In the process, they co-operated, with commendable effectiveness, with a spontaneously organised resistance movement of unparalleled magnitude.

Foreign observers have compared this achievement of the Indian armed forces to the German *blitzkrieg* of the Second World War. *The Sunday Times* of London, which had reporters on all the fronts, wrote on 12 December, "It took only 12 days for the Indian Army to smash its way to Dacca, an achievement reminiscent of the German *blitzkrieg* across France in 1940. The strategy was the same: speed, ferocity and flexibility." The previously rated second-class military machine of a developing country had planned, directed, managed and executed an operation of incredible complexity with consummate skill and sophistication.

One general misconception must be cleared from the beginning. There has been much speculation as to why the Pakistan Army "collapsed" in Bangla Desh: whereas the fact is that there was nothing like a general collapse. In many places, as at Hilli, Jamalpur, Khulna and other strongholds, the enemy put up bitter resistance—often having to be physically destroyed before the post could be captured. To be sure, in certain cases such as Jessore and Mymensingh, the enemy withdrew from their defences before the main assault could be put in—but by and large they fought hard. There were many defended towns still holding out when the surrender was announced—as at Mainamati (Comilla), Khulna, Dinajpur, Saidpur and (a portion of) Sylhet. Had our Army based its plan on capturing these strongholds, the fighting would have lasted many weeks more. The real achievement of Eastern Command was that it outwitted the enemy by swift movement and by-passing tactics over ground that was previously thought to be inoperable; before the enemy could realise what had hit them our columns were converging on Dacca. The war was over before the battles were won.

Certainly there were moral factors involved too. After months of brutality, looting and raping the Pakistani Army, from the highest commanders to the men in the ranks, had become partly dehumanised. Only those who saw at first-hand the evidence of the "dark ages" behaviour of that once-fine Army can understand the debasing process that had shorn the Pakistanis of professional mettle. In almost all the cantonments and defensive strongholds, hundreds of young women had been kept in barracks and bunkers for mass sexual assault; in many cases they were bayonetted or shot every few days as replacements were brought in. Mass slaughter of Bengalis was carried out until the very last days; burning and looting of inhabited areas had become standard procedure—all by order of the omnipotent Special Intelligence Service in Dacca. When these soldiers met on the field of battle a corps of gentlemen such as the Indian officers and jawans proved themselves to be, a moral ascendancy was established which must surely have had a psychological effect on their quality. Foreign observers in Dacca, who reported craven behaviour on the part of Pakistanis during the last few days of the campaign, are witnesses to this degeneration.

This moral disintegration, however, was evident in the conduct of the Pakistan Army as a whole rather than in individual battles. The collapse was that of the *image* of the army: units and brigade groups often resisted ferociously.

The main reason why they were vanquished so decisively and so quickly is because they were thrown off balance by the vastly superior direction and execution of the offensive—"a classic case of the plan that worked against the plan that did not," as Mr Henry Stanhope of the *Times* of London wrote on 24 December. Or, as the *Sunday Telegraph* of 19 December put it, "India won above all because of a sense of vision, a carefully defined and maintained sense of purpose, with which the leadership, at times inspired, of Mrs Indira Gandhi had imbued her nation".

It is but natural that in this brief history of the war of 1971, emphasis has been laid on the war in the east, the liberation of Bangla Desh. This does not, however, detract from the achievements on the western front, where the Indian forces held the enemy at bay while Eastern Command set about completing its task. The heaviest and bloodiest battles of the war were fought along the border between India and Pakistan in the west. Both material losses and casualties were heavier in the west than in the east.

From the very beginning of the Bangla Desh crisis, when the horrifying extent and degree of the deliberate policy of extermination enforced by Pakistan became known to the world, the sympathies of the democratic people of the west—from whom India has chosen to adopt the democratic form of government and the values inherent in the open society—have always been with the people of Bangla Desh and her principal supporter. In Britain, even the government, for many years more sympathetic to Pakistan than to India, did not hesitate to condemn the atrocities: in France, the country which two hundred years ago contributed to the idea of western democracy the notion of egalitarianism, the reaction was similar. In the United States, where Asian affairs do not normally excite widespread interest, there have been demonstrations of unprecedented involvement in and support of the Bangla Desh people—not only by the young, the academic world, the liberals and certain sections of the conservatives but also from members of the administration, officials and American diplomats abroad. Rarely has a head of state been so openly criticised, abused, rejected, as has President Nixon over his ill-advised (and, in the end, impotent) anti-Indian stand. And now, finally, after the recent Anderson Syndicated Publications, disclosing Kissinger-Nixon views, the responsibility for official American anti-Indian attitudes focuses solely on the White House. As *Washington Evening Star* columnist Milton Viorst wrote on January 11, the cable sent by Mr Keating, US Ambassador in New Delhi, to Mr Rogers, US Secretary of State, disputing Dr Kissinger's version of events leading up to the Indo-Pakistani war could only imply that the White House was putting out misleading statements. Mr Viorst said that Mr Keating's message would "go down as the most revealing of everyday official duplicity (in Washington).":

For India, this wealth of support has been a source of strength and gratification—immeasurably greater in extent than was her disappointment at the opposition she met at the United Nations. Those states who, misguided or under pressure, voted against the liberation of Bangla Desh, will have to wait until a smiling and "golden" Bengali nation emerges from the ruins of Pakistan's former colony—to judge whether they were right or wrong.

CHAPTER I

Backdrop to Bangla Desh

*I am overwhelmed by a deep sense of gratitude to Almighty
Allah and to my beloved countrymen—the students, workers
and peasants—for the unprecedented victory of the Awami
League, both in the National and Provincial elections. I
warmly thank the people for having given an historic verdict
in favour of our Six-point Programme. We pledge to implement this verdict. There can be no constitution except one
which is based on the Six-point Programme.*

The Pakistani National Assembly election of 17 December
1970 awarded Sheikh Mujibur Rehman and the Awami League
an overwhelming victory. To the average newspaper reader,
lacking personal involvement in the area, this news may not
have come as a surprise—but it did not make an impact either.
A number, undoubtedly, briefly cheered Sheikh Mujib's
victory in the atavistic fashion which automatically supports
the underdog. Only those with empirical knowledge of sub-
continental affairs and, perhaps, a few other super-prescients
could sense an ominous development in the election outcome:
but even they could not have predicted that the massacre of
a million lives and the ruin of ten million others, the escalation
of Asian tension nearing the level of super-power confrontation,
a major sub-continental war and the emergence of a nation
of 75 million people would devolve in the ensuing twelve
months.
The election results were startlingly decisive in an age when
nations have been governed by leaders elected with perilously

slim margins or, on occasion, on technical interpretation of electoral law. The wide margin is generally a luxury reserved for leaders of totalitarian states. The figures in the Pakistani National and Provincial elections speak for themselves. Of the contested seats in the National Assembly 167 were won by the Awami League and a combined total of 146 by the other ten political parties. It must be noted that of the 167 Awami League seats, 160 were from (then) East Pakistan, the remaining seven being "Indirectly Elected Women's seats". The runner-up was the Pakistan People's Party whose 88 seats constituted the only other solid voting bloc. The other eight parties gained "blocs" ranging in number from one to fourteen. The National Awami Party, West Pakistan's ideological "cousin-brother" to the Awami League, polled seven seats. The results for the contested seats in the Eastern Provincial Assembly must be an example of every politician's cherished dream: of 310 seats the Awami League polled 298; four other parties gained a combined total of five and the Independents won seven.

The Awami League's landslide victory primarily represented the growing Bengali resentment of economic and political domination by the military government in the west and, secondarily, a favourable reaction to Sheikh Mujib's charisma—and his Six-point Programme. This widely known programme, first announced by the Sheikh in 1966, was a working paper to alleviate the economic disparities between the two Pakistans and, thus, stem the growing discontent of the eastern wing. Once again statistics must speak—and the Six-point Programme responds:

1. The Constitution should provide for a federated Pakistan in the true sense on the basis of the Lahore resolution and for a Parliamentary form of Government based on the supremacy of a duly elected legislature on the basis of universal adult franchise.
2. The Federal Government shall deal only with two subjects—defence and foreign affairs—with all residuary subjects vested in the federating states.

3. There should be either two separate freely convertible currencies for the two wings or one currency with two separate Reserve Banks to prevent inter-wing flight of capital.
4. The power of taxation and revenue collection shall be vested in the federating units. The Federal Government will receive a share to meet its financial obligations. .
5. Economic disparities between the two wings shall disappear through a series of economic, fiscal and legal reforms.
6. A militia or para-military force must be created in East Pakistan, which at present has no defence of its own.

The foregoing demands reflected the need to balance the following statistics: the eastern wing, while responsible for 75 per cent of the export and foreign earnings, consumed only 20–30 per cent of imported goods; of development funds, the burgeoning industries of the western side representing 40 per cent of the population, received 77 per cent of the input. The disparity between the per capita income in the West and East was 62 per cent and steadily increasing every year: yet, the price of rice, the staple food of the Bengali, was four times as high in East Bengal as in West Pakistan.

The prestige services echoed this imbalance in their selection policies, West Pakistan claiming 94 per cent of the Civil Services, 85 per cent of the Foreign Service and 95 per cent of the Army. The eastern sector was similarly excluded from the benefits of or participation in—on the professional level—the services of Agriculture, Education, Medicine and Welfare.

Sheikh Mujib's involvement with and espousal of the Bengali cause began during his student days at the University of Dacca where, in 1951, he witnessed Liaquat Ali Khan's public support of Urdu as the national language of Pakistan. His career, jail sentences served for his cause alternating with political advancement, brought him finally to his position of Chief of the Awami League—a position from which, not unnaturally, he looked forward to correcting the civil and

economic imbalances between the Eastern and Western
sectors of Pakistan.

Unfortunately these disparities springing as they did from
deeply ingrained ethnic attitudes and perpetuated by economic
opportunism, were not amenable to cure simply by corrective
legislation. East Bengal with equal rights and economic parity
would, with its larger population and foreign exchange earnings, have been dominant over the West. This potential situation, proposed and outlined in the Six-point Programme, was
an intolerable threat to the military and ruling elite of West
Pakistan.

It was at times difficult to comprehend just how this situation
had arisen—that the down-trodden, colonised people of East
Bengal should be in a position to pose a threat to the mighty
military dictators of the "ruling" nation. Until only a few
weeks before the elections, it would have seemed absurd
to suggest that Yahya Khan, supported by American and
Chinese policies, could be made to feel insecure by the East
Bengali politicians whom the West Pakistanis had consistently
ignored for so many years.

The genesis of the crisis, in fact, lay in the illusion that
Islam was a stronger binding factor than cultural heritage.
Yahya Khan and his army were to kill a million Muslims
before that myth was finally exploded.

The vision of a Muslim Nation on the sub-continent survived many mutations before its geographically schizoid
realisation in 1947. The Lahore Resolution, in 1940, is an
ambiguous document, perhaps representing the uncertainties
of its drafters. It was however, the first official proposal of a
Muslim state or, notably, *states* based on the principle of
Muslim majority in geographically contiguous areas. Three
sovereign states were specifically envisaged; Pakistan in the
north-west, Hyderabad in the south and East Bengal or
"Banga-i-Islam".

The primary objective of the Muslim League was a legislative
framework in which the Muslim community would be assured
of absolute parity with its Hindu counterpart after indepen-

dence. The plans advanced ranged from the crackpot and visionary to the politic. But a firm determination to weld a national Islamic unity between the north-west and the east seems not to have predominated. A loose federation of all sub-continental states supporting separate but equal Muslim and Hindu nations was (if barely) acceptable to the Muslim League as late as in 1946, in conference with the Cabinet Mission. The Indian National Congress, however, suspecting collaboration between the Muslim League and the British to delay independence, decided that partition was not too high a price to pay for the immediate end of the colonial era.

No amount of true devotion to Islam could serve to bridge the ethnic and cultural distance between the West Pakistani and the East Bengali. The former is influenced by the proselytising *jehad* spirit emanating from Mecca; the latter by the gentler conviction which characterises Islam in South-East Asia. The former is active, the latter passive—and Islam, of the major world creeds, is perhaps the least tolerant of religious passivity. With even their approach to their mutual religion marked by diversant attitudes it is no wonder that, considering ethnic, cultural and geographic gaps, the two Pakistans found their marriage of convenience uncomfortable from the start.

Jinnah, the "founding father", aware of these dichotomies and conscious of the significant percentage of non-Muslims remaining within Pakistani territory, had, after partititon, to urge a secular sense of national identity. Thus, at the outset, a paradox arose; two completely different peoples were welded together in a geographically incongruous union on the tenuous principle of common religion—and then told that creed should not be the primary motivation of national loyalty.

This situation, while curious, is understandable. Jinnah sought to avoid any further exacerbation of the communal tensions in the wake of the 1947 riots. Subsequent leaders, however, in efforts to allay growing Bengali discontent, relied heavily on the theme of Muslim unity—particularly in its "them or us" aspect *vis a vis* India. The emphasis on Islam was intended to downplay the importance of the internal problems and dissensions which plagued Pakistan during the eleven years between partition and the commencement of Ayub Khan's military regime in 1958. These problems, by no means confined to the economic realm, included: the language agitations triggered by the west wing's longstanding refusal to confer national status on any language other than Urdu; the separatist sentiments, within West Pakistan itself, of Sind and Baluchistan; and the question of regional or popular apportionment of seats in the national legislature. The fact that during this period seven different governments came successively to power (and went—none by the ballot box) reflects the cumulative instability caused by all of these.

In October 1958 the military, traditionally and universally impatient of politicians and the tortuous procedures of government-by-consent, took matters into its own hands. The occasional examples of military dictatorships which have commenced with benevolent aspirations—the desire to order a country's economic and social affairs—have rarely ended that way. Certainly the mentality of command and obedience inherent in any army and its tight organisational infrastructure seems temptingly well-equipped to undertake and carry out reforms, by-passing the delays and pitfalls of bureaucracy. Unfortunately the 1958 coup had no social programme to implement. What it did have were upcoming general elections and a threatened Bengali victory to avoid. General (subsequently President) Ayub Khan, soon to emerge as the strong man in the internecine struggles within the coup, led his country's government for the next decade on a negative rather than positive basis.

The Ayub regime, without regard to its failure or success in an historical perspective, was characterised by three qualities: the first, obviously, the dominant military voice in national affairs; the second, the gradual turnover of domestic responsibility by military officers to civil servants; the third, a not unusual component of military dictatorship, Ayub's personal assumption of policy responsibility in both the formulative and decisive stages.

Efforts to give the military government a legal armature were made despite Ayub's statement: "My authority is revolution. I have no sanction in law or Constitution". In his policy announcements he reiterated that the people of Pakistan, badly served by politicians, would return in time to a democratic form of government. The *Law Orders,* mitigating the impression of total military dictatorship, were brilliantly devised in the manner of a self-fulfilling prophecy: since no writs could be issued against the Martial Law Administration, any action it took was automatically invested with its own legality.

The martial administration did announce and begin to implement reforms in several areas: land; the economy; education and civil administration. The outcome of these reforms is best judged elsewhere in greater depth, and blame or credit to be assigned for individual projects would, perhaps, be more accurate in a longer historical perspective. Certainly a decade later, whatever progress may have been achieved in West Pakistan, East Bengal had not benefited in any comparable way.

One incidental advantage gained by the military in its adventure in government was removal of the threat of a probable policy of non-alignment in the event of Bengali success at the polls. This threat came uncomfortably close to the Army jugular. A neutral international stance would jeopardise the input of military hardware from countries willing, at any price, to lay the spectre of communism. Also, the minimal number of Bengali officers in the Army assured that, under a military regime, the eastern wing was even further excluded from participation in government.

No revolution is sympathetic to the politics of the establishment it has replaced and, as previously mentioned, the instinct of the soldier is not to love the politician. All political parties, banned when Ayub assumed power, so remained until the 1962 elections when, using the party system as a pipeline to "grassroots" voters, Ayub affiliated himself with the Muslim League. In the intervening years he had established the system of "Basic Democracies"—on paper, at any rate, an admirable

and simple plan of broad-based political participation which
had the net effect of eliminating both the politician and the
political buffer between leader and people. The "Basic Democracies" plus some early success in land reform which won
the support of small landowners (as it were, the bourgeoisie
of agriculture) assured a comfortable election victory for Ayub
in 1962.

With Ayub in undisputed control at the top and "Basic
Democracies" functioning at the district and *tehsil* level
the administration gradually assumed a less martial comple-
xion. At any rate, civilian affairs came to be civilly administered.
This left the Army in a vacuum similar to that of, if less odious
than, the politician. Ayub, not unnaturally exercising his dicta-
torial prerogatives, made the majority of his policy decisions
on his own rather than in consultation with army or other
"authorities". This procedure provides potentially the most
vulnerable aspect of any dictatorship, benevolent or otherwise.
Collective responsibility (and collective guilt) perpetuate themselves for lack of one recognisable villain who can be made the
scape-goat. There is, however, no such thing as the indispens-
able man.

The 1962 Presidential Constitution and the system of indirect
representation, both indicating Ayub's basic distrust of the
people's capacity for self-government, portended the ensuing
course of his administration. Increasingly reluctant, despite
earlier pronouncements, to relinquish power, Ayub was forced
to ever more stringent measures to maintain it. Corruption,
inevitable where power is the end rather than the means,
flourished against a background of increasing administrative
chaos. In the spring of 1969 President Ayub Khan, after a
six months period of mounting popular turmoil, was ousted
and General Yahya Khan, without noticeable reluctance,
came forward to take his place.

Yahya Khan's promises, a breath of fresh air to the post
1967–68 Pakistani scene, nonetheless bore a remarkable
similarity to the Ayub pronouncements a decade earlier.
However, two salient differences soon became apparent bet-

ween Yahya's regime and that of his predecessor: the military, due to its active role in Ayub's removal and Yahya's promotion, resumed martial administration of civil affairs; and Yahya, perhaps profiting from the experience of the former incumbent, made policy decisions in consultation—thus committing his peers to collective responsibility for unforeseen or unpopular results. It has been advanced by some that Yahya—"the best of a brutal bunch"—was perhaps too egalitarian in his acceptance of colleague's advice.

In fact Yahya Khan's aim was to perpetuate the absolute power of the military junta while according it the respectability of democratic approval. From the arrogance of his seat of power, he failed to appreciate the inherent strength of democratic aspirations—particularly in East Bengal. When in 1969 he first announced the specially devised legal framework within which the 1970 elections were to be held, he assumed that none of the opportunistic political parties of Pakistan would ever be able to muster sufficient votes to form a majority government. He even agreed, gratuitously, to the "one-man-one-vote" formula—never imagining it possible that the potential power this gave the 75 millions of East Bengal would ever be realised.

It is not surprising that the election results, which not only gave East Bengal a majority of seats in the National Assembly, but represented massive popular support for the Six-point Programme, were absolutely unacceptable to the military junta in West Pakistan. The acceptance of the election results would mean an end to the junta's veto—and consequently the end of military rule. Pressure was therefore immediately put on Sheikh Mujib to dilute his demands.

The Sheikh, however, was adamant that there be no compromise in either letter or spirit of his programme. As the tension mounted in the ensuing weeks Mr Bhutto, leader of the People's Party, the runner-up, grabbed the opportunity to announce his party's intention of boycotting the upcoming Assembly—thus providing a pretext for the President to postpone the Assembly indefinitely. When on 1 March Yahya Khan's announcement came over the radio, indefinitely postponing the opening of the National Assembly, the people of Bangla Desh were stunned. This breach of faith at the last moment was the supreme act of treachery. The outrage and frustration of the Bengalis erupted in violent demonstrations in Dacca and elsewhere in East Bengal—in many cases leading to clashes between rioters and the police. The Sheikh's message to the people regarding a programme of action for the achievement of "self-determination" did nothing to assuage their outrage. Nothing but independence would do—they could never trust the West Pakistani again.

Bangla Desh was born that day.

Anticipating the reaction in East Bengal, Yahya Khan had already set in motion the only machine he knew of—military force—to deal with the situation. It was going to be swift and harsh. The form of the reaction should not have come as a surprise—rumours everywhere had acquired a martial tone since the President's dissolution, on 21 February, of his civilian cabinet. His subsequent group consultations with top Army officers, including the martial administrators, while less bruited about, were known to a number of people. They were also in line with his policy of shared responsibility. The implementation of any plan to thwart the election results would require, from the military, both full cooperation and collective involvement.

Having ascertained that the military was solidly with him (the few dissenters were discreetly removed from their positions) Yahya was able to move in a more determined fashion. A form of self-censorship was imposed on the press: movements of Army officers were not to be reported except in the context of official government press releases. Using the pretext of the Indo-Pakistani tension following the early February hi-jacking incident (itself, it increasingly appears, a put-up job for this very purpose) he began to mobilise. The armed forces were put on a state of alert and a battalion of the Baluch regiment plus a large supply of ammunition were ordered to Dacca by sea—to arrive in Chittagong on 3 March. Other troops and supplies were shuttled from west to east in a fleet of Pakistan

Air Force *C-130s*. These were intended to bring West Pakistani units in East Bengal up to strength and replace Bengali units being transferred to the west. It was arranged that Pakistan International Airways would airlift troops on a large scale if and when required. Those Bengali officers still in the east found themselves either transferred to rural areas or assigned to routine trivia. Tanks were brought to Dacca from their defensive positions on the Indian border and converted to soft tracks for use on urban roads. All of this was carried out under tight security.

When Yahya's March announcement of the postponement of the Assembly opening sparked the riots in East Bengal the Pakistan Army was ready—prepared for everything except the massive scale and vehemence of the popular reaction. Sheikh Mujib, in an effort to restore some vestige of calm or, at least, constructive purpose, called for a general strike to begin on 2 March. The near unanimous response from all levels of society not only brought the urban routine to a standstill but freed the citizenry to participate in still more demonstrations. A curfew ordered by Pakistan Army's Eastern Command Headquarters was largely ignored and Army patrols firing into the crowds were completely overrun. The Sheikh called for a non-violent, non-cooperation movement. It was, however, too late in the day for non-violence.

Lieut-General Tikka Khan, newly appointed Martial Law Administrator, arrived in Dacca to find a paralysed province: all the usual municipal amenities had ceased to function due to the strike. Significantly, Tikka Khan's predecessor, Admiral Ahsan, appears to have been one of the few officers who disagreed with Yahya's proposals at the Fibruary conclaves.

Sheikh Mujib was *de facto* ruler of East Bengal but never, at this stage, used his charismatic power to urge independence. The mounting intensity of both regional patriotic fervour and the reaction of the Martial Administration, however, made inevitable an early announcement of secession. Mujib had promised an official message on 7 March and the betting was that this occasion would witness East Bengal's declaration of intent to fight for national integrity. It was, as it turned out, no safer a bet than the election returns.

The crowd, one million strong, gathered at the Dacca Racecourse, was disappointed by the subdued quality of Mujib's address. Accustomed to his usual "blood and thunder" style and expecting the declaration of independence which was not forthcoming, they failed to accord him that emotional crescendo which a sure and experienced orator can evoke from a tense crowd. Unaware that the Sheikh had come to the Racecourse directly from an eighteen hour session discussing future plans, strategy and the question of immediate declaration of independence, they were bewildered. During these discussions the Sheikh had fended off increasingly insistent demands from student and "radical" representatives to announce a sovereign Bangla Desh to the world. Older, more committed to working within a legal framework, certainly more vulnerable to that fear of needless bloodshed which accrues with age, Mujib insisted that a satisfactory political solution could be found.

Independence was the central point of these discussions. The students and younger elements present argued that the massive support which the strikes and non-cooperation movement had achieved, argued a popular strength with which the Army, surprised by the magnitude of events and, as yet, not up to full strength in the area, could not cope. Proponents of the more conservative faction argued that the Awami League, as the legally elected majority party, must inevitably be recognised and accorded a measure of international support. In the meantime a rash move or final break would exacerbate the mood of the military forces (if not up to full strength, certainly capable of inflicting widespread damage) beyond handling.

Sober counsel prevailed and an immense body of students enveloped the procession to the Racecourse with their own bitter and disappointed fatalism. "If-ing" is a dangerous thing to commence when dissecting historic events, but one must accord a degree of justice to both sides of the argument over immediate secession. Had the massed crowd in its fervour and commitment marched on the relatively unprepared Eastern Command Headquarters of the Pakistan Army and demanded immediate surrender, Bangla Desh might that day have emerged as a new nation. Certainly a price would have been paid in lives—but it would have been cheaper that that which has ultimately been paid.

The Pakistani Army, understandably tense over its sudden impotence to deal with events, persuaded the President that the deterrent measures previously envisaged would be insufficient to effect his plan. Eastern Command Headquarters was, in short, somewhat disconcerted. Tikka Khan urged 'over-kill' : "Give me enough force and I'll crush them in 48 hours". Yahya, an amateur statesman rather than a politician, reacted in a fashion which reflected the duality of his roles: the President immediately acceded to the thorough military suppression of the Bengali "uprising"; the General, aware that the forces then under Eastern Command were inadequate to the situation, played for time. Time was needed to transport a sufficient military presence to quell this and (with the "final solution" approach) any other secessionist tendencies.

The massive airlift of troops began and contingency battle plans were ordered into effect. Retrospectively, it is clear that the Army argued for a minimum of nineteen days to complete preparations for the definitive crack-down in East Bengal—and to provide this Yahya resorted to subterfuge. On 6 March, addressing the nation by radio, he announced the new date for the Assembly opening—25 March. Time could be bought only by a convincing appearance of sincere negotiations with the Awami League. Yahya was eminently successful in this ruse—whether by his own skill, the Sheikh's naivete or a combination of the two. The negotiations began under Yahya's control and served his purpose.

For some reason the postponement of the date of the Assembly session ha been completely misunderstood...this misunderstanding has become the rallying cry for the forces of disorder.... While realising that an application of adequate force can effectively bring the situation under control I have deliberately ordered the authorities in East Pakistan to use the absolute minimum force required .... I have consequently decided that the inaugural session of the National Assembly will take place on 25 March.

Martial tone and ultimate intent were clearly discernible in the address:

Finally, let me make it absolutely clear that no matter what happens as long as I am in command of the Pakistan Armed Forces and Head of State, I will ensure complete and absolute integrity of Pakistan.... It is the duty of the Pakistan Armed Forces to ensure the integrity, solidarity and security of Pakistan, a duty in which they have never failed.

Sheikh Mujib's reaction to this announcement was contained within the framework of his four-point demand made at the famous Racecourse address the following day. Perhaps the modesty of the "demands" accounted in part for the crowd's tepid response.

1. The withdrawal of Martial Law
2. Sending of troops back to barracks
3. Inquiry into killings (resultant from demonstrations)
4. Transfer of power to the elected representatives of the people.

The paradox then: the Sheikh was clearly aware of the military buildup within East Bengal; of the destructive compulsions and capabilities of that military body unleashed on the Bengali civilian populace; that civilian deaths incurred in the name of mob control would be numerous and without any recourse except retaliatory measures which would further exacerbate the situation; and aware that a showdown was imminent for which Pakistan Army's Eastern Command Headquarters would be adequately prepared. Why did he not re-enforce the general strikes and autonomous administration policies with some sort of defensive contingency plan ? The

motivational unanimity of East Bengal during this period
was unparalleled in history. All levels of society participated
in implementing the strikes and were prepared to venture
physical action to further their goals.

In his blundering, blustering way Yahya Khan had decided
that the only way to save the situations was to break up the
base from which Mujibur Rehman and the Awami League
drew their support, particularly the intellectuals and the elite—
and, of course, the Hindu minority. He had imported the
"Butcher of Baluchistan", Tikka Khan, to do the job for him.

Between Yahya's announcement of the 25 March opening
of the Assembly and that date he, through the ploy of lengthy
negotiations, diverted Mujib from his actual intent. The Sheikh,
in turn, managed to keep the Bengalis if not docile, at least
cooperative with his policies. As Mascarenhas in *The Rape
of Bangla Desh* has said of the negotiations which were never
meant to negotiate: "The most notable feature was the fact
that they never broke down." On 25 March the Army was
prepared, the stage set. The need for this elaborate pretence
was over.

He arrested Mujib, arranged for his own getaway to West
Pakistan and then gave the infamous order to Tikka Khan:
"Sort them out".

Tikka Khan, who had started life as an illiterate soldier in
the Pakistan Army (and, despite his rank, never really
graduated to any higher standard of intellect or culture) believed that he had the best solution to the problem. He would
wipe out Dacca University—the centre for the dissemination
of liberal and democratic ideas, kill a few thousand intellectuals and professionals of the middle classes, let loose his
soldiery on a rampage in the urban areas to cow the people
into submission—and thus preserve the junta's colonial rule
over East Bengal. He embarked upon the grisly task of mass
slaughter, mass destruction, looting and organised rape on
the night of 25 March.

The total resistance that the people of East Bengal offered
against this rule of terror, the resistance that gave birth to

the Bangla Desh Liberation Force (which eventually became
the Mukti Bahini) was something neither Tikka Khan nor
Yahya Khan expected—or really comprehended. As this resistance grew, more and more Pakistani forces were flown in from
the west—until the Pakistan Army strength eventually increased
to 4½ infantry divisions and more than 25,000 other military
and para-military forces. With every extra contingent flown
in, Pakistan's overall strategic situation deteriorated—but the
bungling, second-rate generals of the junta failed to appreciate
the danger.

When the military leaders saw that there was no reaction
from India, and the resistance movement continued to grow
in strength, the "elitocide" campaign was expanded in scope
to one of genocide and mass eviction of refugees to Indian
territory. The troops fanned out from Dacca and other conton-
ments to the countryside, burning villages and slaughtering their
inhabitants. The Hindus and other Awami League supporters
were singled out for special treatment—but all Bengalis were
considered fair game.

Towards the end of April the refugees began to pour over
the border into India. First they came in their hundreds of
thousands then in their millions. Still the rampage went on.
The Liberation Forces had been dealt a blow in the first few
battles, when they were still relatively unorganised and leaderless. Pakistan's Army had had it all its own way: but its generals were too insensate to realise what the outcome would be—
the awakening of the sleeping giant that was India.

CHAPTER II

The Threat to India

Soon after Pakistan launched its repressive campaign in East Bengal, it became clear that the political and strategic implications would not remain confined to that country alone but would inevitably engulf the whole sub-continent. Quite apart from the question of the threat to security, the events in East Bengal since mid-February had resulted in creating a widespread sense of political commitment in India. Resolutions in the Lok Sabha and the State Legislatures, the formation of a Bangla Desh government-in-exile on Indian territory, the sanctuary given to members of the Mukti Fouj and political leaders—all these developments had created a sense of national commitment that could no longer be ignored.

The deepest concern, however, was the threat to India's security. It is true that after the border tension following the hi-jacking incident of February 1971 had died down, there was no danger of immediate aggression; but national security in its wider and more long-term sense involves factors beyond those of immediate threats.

The aim of national security in the more sophisticated sense is to protect internal values, primarily by political and diplomatic endeavour but if necessary by the threat of force (deterrence) or, in the extreme, by the *use* of force. As a concept national security includes defence but has a much wider purview. As Walter Lippman has defined it: "A nation has security when it does not have to sacrifice its legitimate interests to avoid war and is able, if challenged, to maintain them by war." It is when the last contingency arises—that is,

38   *The Lightning Campaign*

the necessity to protect our internal values and external interests by waging war—that national security planning comes into play and eventually leads to defence strategy.

Among the internal values that the Union of India has to safeguard is its desire to achieve and maintain a sense of national integration based on secularism, and to preserve the democratic character of its political and social fabric. Both of these were threatened, in the aftermath of Pakistan's campaign of deliberate genocide in Bangla Desh and with the continuing influx of refugees evicted by the Pakistani forces. The presence of these millions of refugees aside from imposing an intolerable economic burden would create unbearable tensions in West Bengal and Tripura—states in which accentuated social disparities had already caused a near break-down of the administration and where there already existed the danger of revolutionary strife. In addition, there was the dangerous potential for nation-wide disruption of communal harmony.

Furthermore, it was becoming increasingly evident that if there was to be no political and military reaction from India to support the uprising in Bangla Desh, the nature of the insurgency, which had so far been entirely nationalistic, would become more and more extremist oriented—and thus have long-term repercussions on the situation in West Bengal and elsewhere. The mass eviction of refugees was a deliberate act of demographic aggression. It constituted a clear threat to our national security.

Understandably, there was a reluctance on the part of the Indian government to solve the problem by recourse to military action. Such a course—even at a controlled level—would carry with it dangers of escalation to all-out war with Pakistan and, consequently, the possibility of Chinese intervention as well as military support by the United States. In order fully to understand the government's dilemma in this respect it is necessary to review the strategic situation in India during the early part of 1971—as also the state of preparedness of the Indian armed forces.

After the experience of the Indo-Pakistan war of 1965,

during which the Chinese had threatened India with military action, it became obvious that in any future confrontation with either Pakistan or China, the other could be expected to pose a simultaneous threat in support of its ally. The defence policy of India had therefore to be re-adjusted to one of maintaining a capability to conduct a two-front war simultaneously. Another factor that was highlighted—both during the 1962 and the 1965 operations—was that when actually faced with war India found herself too dependent upon aid procurement from Western powers; and that she should not depend on continuation of such aid if the Western powers concerned were unsympathetic to Indian aims.

In the wake of the 1962 war against China, the Government of India had announced an expansion programme for the armed forces. In 1964, this was incorporated in a five year Defence Plan amounting to an outlay of Rs 5,000 crores—for which the United States and the United Kingdom had promised support in the way of grants and credits. The Plan envisaged the expansion of the Army to a manpower ceiling of 8,25,000 men and a programme for the modernisation of equipment; the expansion of the Air Force to 45 squadrons equipped with modern aircraft; the establishment of production facilities for the purpose of substantially reducing dependence on external sources of supply; and the expansion of the military research and development organisation. Subsequently, though the Soviet Union provided India with many items of equipment—transport aircraft, helicopters and light (*PT 76*) tanks—and fulfilled its undertaking regarding the establishment of the *MIG 21* project in India, the United States withheld its aid programme after the 1965 war and the Five Year Plan remained unfulfilled.

When it became necessary to recast the 1965 plan without reliance on the United States, India again turned to the Soviet Union. From the Russians she acquired large quantities of modern armour, field artillery, many squadrons of fighter-bomber aircraft (*Sukhoi 7*), mobile radar and other items of modern weapons and equipment. Much of this procurement

programme, however, was an interim measure pending production plans going into full operation.

India embarked upon a defence programme whereby she
would, over the next ten years, move into the field of spohis-
ticated technology. Ordnance factories for the production of
propellants and explosives were completed without the ori-
ginally promised American assistance. There was a marked
expansion in the production of electronic and sophisticated
air defence ground environment equipment including high
speed computers, the *Mig 21* supersonic interceptor and the
indigenously developed *HF 24* ground attack aircraft with a
successor already on the planning board

The Indian Army was to be equipped with a new field gun
after nearly thirty years of the 25 pounder—a major achievement. It acquired two types of anti-tank missiles, and initiated projects for their indigenous manufacture. For the Air
Observation role for the artillery, it was decided to produce
helicopters in the country. The Navy acquired submarines,
the *Sea-Cat* (surface-to-air) missile and rocket boats—as well
as various low-level anticraft missiles under evaluation for
adoption.

Although expansion and re-equipment programmes were
proceeding smoothly, the Bangla Desh crisis blew up before
they could be fully realised. In the Army, manpower provi-
sioning had not been fully achieved and many units were
still under strength. Some armoured regiments had not completed raising and re-equipping: there were shortfalls in administrative and logistical units required for the conduct of
mobile operations. In the Air Force, the production programme
for *MIG 21* fighters had still not gone into full swing and lack
of spares had reduced some squadrons to a state of low serviceability. In the Navy also, re-equipment projects had not
yet been completed. A few more months of crash programming were required before the armed forces could be brought
up to full war readiness.

More serious than that was the upset in the Army's balance
of forces caused by demands for internal security. Two divi-

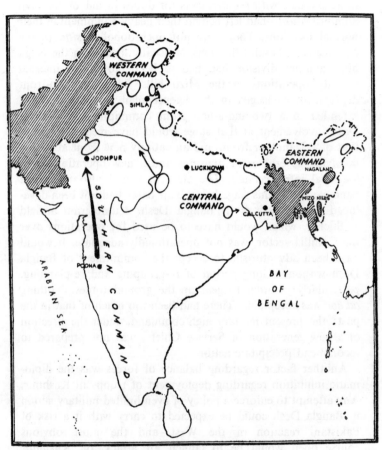

BOUNDARIES ARE APPROXIMATE AND NOT TO SCALE

Force Orientations in early 1971

sions had been deployed in West Bengal and though they were physically close to the Bangla Desh border, the formations—in accordance with requirements for duties in aid of the civil administration—had left behind their heavy equipment in their normal locations. They were not operational *in situ*. In the extreme east, besides the division usually located in the Naga hills, another division had had to be deployed for internal security operations in the Mizo hills. Thus the two-front deployment envisaged in the defence plan had already been extended to a two-and-a-half front commitment: a Bangla Desh involvement at that stage would have meant the addition of yet another front, and an entirely new front at that—involving several extra divisions and a new operational and logistical infrastructure. The air arm would also find itself handicapped at this stage because air bases had not been developed for operations in Bangla Desh. Kumbigram airfield at Silchar, which would have to be used for operations over the Comilla sector, was not operationally adequate. It would have been adventuristic to accept the commitment of Bangla Desh without a long period of re-grouping and re-planning, particularly in order to gear up the ground forces. Nothing *ad hoc* was acceptable. There had been too much of that in the past: the present military high command, under the direction of a new generation of Service Chiefs, was not prepared to recommend precipitate action.

Another factor regarding balance of forces was the diplomatic inhibition regarding deployment of troops in Kashmir. Any attempt to enforce a policy of even limited military action in Bangla Desh could be expected to carry with it a risk of Pakistani reaction in the West—and the most obvious course open would be to launch an attack on Kashmir. Adhering, as she always has done to the terms of the Cease-Fire Agreement of 1948, India had not deployed any extra troops within the territory of Jammu and Kashmir. Her lines of communication from Pathankot to Jammu and from Jammu forward to the Rajouri-Poonch sector thus lay open to disruption by a surprise Pakistani offensive. Before adopting a course of military action in the east, India would have to induct at least one more division to safeguard her lines of communication (l of c).

Another consideration was the strategic meteorological disadvantage of April-May. The monsoons were expected over the eastern part of the sub-continent; the heavy rains and cloudy weather would render the ground as well as the air over it unsuitable for full scale operations, defensive or offensive. At the same time, along the northern borders, the passes would open with the approach of summer, thus facilitating Chinese intervention.

Any operation in support of Bangla Desh would have to be spearheaded by the freedom fighters of that country. As explained in the next chapter, the Mukti Fouj (or the Mukti Bahini, as the re-grouped, all-arms force was subsequently re-named) had taken a hard beating in the battles following the Pakistani treachery of 25 March. It would take a period of re-organisation, re-fitting and re-training before the Bahini could play a key-role in any projected military action.

From all points of view, the spring of 1971 was clearly not the time for India's armed forces to operate at maximum advantage. Three conditions had to be fulfilled before India could assume influence over Bangla Desh policy by recourse to military action with its implicit risk of all-out war:

1. She would have to complete her expansion and re-equipment programme as well as re-group her armed forces and re-plan deployment;
2. She would have to wait until the Mukti Bahini had acquired a degree of operational capability;
3. She would have to wait until such time as the Chinese threat of intervention was minimised both by diplomatic action and by choosing the most favourable season.

The terrain in Bangla Desh is not dry enough for mobile operations until mid-November. On the northern borders the passes are not snowbound until even later in the winter (albeit there were indications already that Communist China was being gradually brought into the fold of the comity of nations, where restraint and responsibility would automatically be imposed). As for the preparedness of the armed forces, five or six months of crash programming would bring them to a pitch of operational readiness: and it would take at least three to four months to raise a sizeable and effective force for the Mukti Bahini. All indications, therefore, pointed to November 1971 as being the earliest when India could assume a positive military posture in support of a Bangla Desh policy.

India's Armed Forces

According to published figures, the Indian Army at the beginning of 1971, with a total strength of just over eight and a quarter lakhs of men, was organised into thirteen infantry divisions, ten mountain divisions, several independent infantry brigades, two parachute brigades, one armoured division and some independent armoured brigades. It is pertinent to point out that an Indian mountain division is basically organised on the lines of an infantry division except that in artillery support and in logistical compliments it has weapons and transport more suitable for deployment and movement in mountainous terrain. Mountain divisions can, with re-adjustments in medium and field artillery and additional transport, be operationally deployed in the plains.

India's infantry formations are equipped with the 7.62 mm self-loading *Ishapore* rifles, 7.62 mm light and medium machine guns, 81 mm and 120 mm mortars—all indigenously produced. The mountain divisions depend upon artillery support by pack mountain guns (the 75/24 Indian produced gun and the Yugoslav 76 mm gun). Infantry divisions are supported mainly by the time-honoured 25 pr gun, some Russian 100 mm field guns and the 130 mm medium guns (replacing the old 5.5 in mediums). The heavy gun is the 7.2 in howitzer. The anti-aircraft artillery consists of the old 40 mm 6-6-(radar controlled) gun.

In armour, it is estimated that the Indian Army increased its strength since 1965 by about 450 *T-55* and *T-56* Russian medium tanks, 300 *Vijayanta* (Indian produced) tanks mounting the powerful 105 mm gun and the faithful *Centurions,* which though obsolescent are more than a match for Pakistani (United States supplied) *Pattons* (as was demonstrated at Khem Karan in 1965). Its light armour consists of the *AMX-13* French tank carrying a fairly powerful 75 mm gun and the Russian *PT-76s,* a big lumbering amphibious armoured vehicle with limited fire-power but invaluable in a reconnaissance role, particularly in riverine terrain.

The Indian Air Force, with a strength of about 625 combat aircraft and a total of 90,000 men, has been considerably expanded and modernised since 1965. It now includes seven squadrons of *MIG-21* Supersonic (Mach 2) intercepter fighters, five squadrons of *Sukhoi-7* fighter bombers, seven squadrons of (indigenous) *Gnat* interceptors, six squadrons of *Hunter* fighter bombers, two squadrons of *HF-24* trans-sonic fighters and three squadrons of *Canberra* bombers. Radar surveillance and communication systems for the air arm have been considerably improved since 1965—and surface-to-air anti-aircraft missile systems around important targets in India have been established.

The Indian Navy has also been expanded since 1965, the present manpower strength being about 40,000. The main units are one aircraft carrier (the *Vikrant*), two cruisers, three destroyers, two destroyer escorts, five *Peyta* class patrol vessels, four *F*-class (Russian) ocean-going submarines and some landing craft and minesweeping vessels.

Territorially, the Army is organised into four commands. Western command consists of three army corps of a total of thirteen infantry and one armoured division and some armoured brigades. (This includes the reserve corps normally located in Central India but earmarked for operations on the Western front). Western Command also has two mountain divisions facing the Himalayan front from Ladakh to the Simla sector. Central Command's operational responsibility is

in the central-northern sector of the Himalayas. Eastern
Command (now) consists of three army corps—and its responsibilities extend to the Sikkim, Bhutan and NEFA sectors in
the North, the Naga and Mizo Hills and (before the operations)
the East Bengal border. Southern Command's areas of operational responsibility are in the Kutch sector and in Rajasthan.

The Air Force is organised into four commands—the
Western, Central and Eastern Operational commands and
Maintenance Command.

The Navy now has two fleets—one each for the Eastern
and Western coasts.

Pakistan Armed Forces

The Pakistan Army had, in early 1971, twelve infantry
divisions, two armoured divisions and an armoured brigade.
Out of these, one infantry division was deployed in East Bengal
but later strengthened to four divisions. Two extra divisions
began raising last summer to replace the divisions moved
to the eastern wing—but were not fully operational when
hostilities broke out.

Pakistan Air Force consisted of six squadrons of *MIG-19*
(supersonic) interceptors, six squadrons of *Sabre* (US) fighters,
one squadron of *Mirage III* supersonic fighter, two squadrons
of *B-57* bombers and one squadron of *IL-28* bombers—in
all seventeen combat squadrons. Of these, only one squadron
of *Sabres* was located in East Bengal.

Pakistan Navy consisted of four submarines, one light
cruiser, two destroyers, three destroyer escorts, two fast
frigates and four patrol boats.

Pakistan's para-military forces numbered some 2,50,000
men—located mainly for border duties similar to those of
our Border Security Force.

It is pertinent that whereas the Pakistan Army recruited
very few East Bengalis (less than 10 per cent) their Air Force
and Navy had a larger percentage—some 20 to 30 per cent in
both Services. This must have caused a serious handicap when
war eventually broke out.

Of the Pakistani armed forces, one division of four brigades (14 PAK Division) was normally located in East Bengal. The only heavy elements available to this division were an armoured regiment (about 50 *Chaffee* tanks) and a few artillery units. Air support was provided by one squadron of *Sabre* fighters, some helicopters and various light transport aircraft. The East Pakistan Rifles (the Border Security Force) consisted of about 20,000 men—mixed West Pakistanis and Bengalis, but commanded mainly by Pakistani officers. By early March this garrison was reinforced by rapid and secret induction of two divisions from the western wing—though not with its full artillery compliment. Thereafter the build-up continued until in October four infantry divisions (totalling some 42 battalions) in Bangla Desh as well as 20,000 or more West Punjab Rangers, had been inducted to replace the East Pakistan Rifles.

Military Preparations, March-April

Towards the end of February 1971, following the tension created by the incident of the blowing up of the hi-jacked Indian Airlines aircraft on Lahore airfield, some precautionary moves had taken place on the Western border. Since the incident did not escalate any further, most of the forces sent up to their operational posts were brought back to their peace stations during March. Hardly had these disengagement moves been completed than the Bangla Desh crisis developed.

No strategic moves were undertaken by our armed forces during the first few weeks of the campaign of repression. The Bangla Desh Liberation Army, formed spontaneously from elements of the East Bengal Regiment, the East Pakistan Rifles and the Police, were known to be fighting the Pakistan Army—and our press reports contained highly optimistic reports of their successes. The only aid given to them at this stage was to supply them with small arms—presumably through the Border Security Forces, whenever contact was made with the freedom fighters along our borders.

Both the brutality and the military capacity of the Pakistan Army was underestimated in India—even in government circles. Inured to a democratic and tolerant political and social environment, it was difficult to believe that the mass killing in Dacca was not just an isolated act of butchery but the first step in a calculated and ruthless policy of extermination of certain sections of East Bengal society as well as the deliberate eviction of millions of the minority community. It was not until the genocide campaign was in full swing that the enormity of the horrors had full impact on India.

That was the first mistake. The next was to believe that the unorganised and often leaderless groups of freedom fighters could by themselves combat the ruthless efficiency with which the Pakistani Army set about its extermination campaign.

Yahya Khan's treachery in planning the holocaust even while affecting to hold negotiations with Sheikh Mujibur Rehman and the build up of military forces between mid-February and end-March had been a well kept secret. India was not to know of these measures until some time after the events. Consequently, when reports were received of the blowing up of bridges, the disruption of road and rail communications and highly exaggerated accounts of guerilla successes, a completely wrong appreciation of their military potential was made. There were expectations that Dacca and Comilla having been isolated from the main port, Chittagong, Pakistani garrisons in the capital, in the interior of the country and in the border outposts would be logistically hamstrung— and that their predicament would grow worse with the onset of the monsoons.

The Bangla Desh Liberation Forces, by now styled the Mukti Fouj, were also guilty of overestimating their capacity. They had done more than anyone had expected them to do—motivated beyond historical precedent. But lacking higher direction and carried away by their initial successes, they grew overbold and began to take on the regular forces in pitched battles.

Pakistan's Army in the east was *not* hamstrung. It had built up stocks for just such a contingency—and in any case it was not fighting a war of heavy logistical requirements. Although the Pakistanis used their artillery and aircraft to blast civilians, women and children—wherever they could find a worthwhile kill target—the expenditure of ammunition was not at combat scale.

The Mukti Fouj was armed mainly with rifles, submachine guns and, in some groups, machine guns: captured mortars, leave alone field artillery, were few and far between. For the greater part battles against the Fouj entailed mostly small-arms expenditure, with minimum artillery support. Under such conditions, the Pakistan regular forces could continue to conduct operations for a considerable period—requiring minimum logistical support, which could be provided by a combination of air supply, water-borne transport and, wherever possible, road and rail communications. There could be no great hope of a successful liberation campaign conducted by the Fouj by itself.

The nature of the Bangla Desh insurgency and its political and military implications were not always clearly understood by India's policy makers. Even after the Mukti Bahini had resiled from their early set-backs, re-equipped and re-trained, its exact role in the scheme of things was not at first correctly appreciated. It was felt at one time that somehow "guerilla warfare" conducted by the Bahini, given a modicum of support from India in the way of border sanctuaries, arms and ammunition, co-ordination and training, would be sufficient eventually to defeat the Pakistani army and liberate Bangla Desh. This kind of optimistic appraisal was further encouraged both by glowing press reports regarding "liberated areas" occupied by Mukti Bahini forces and propaganda reports and statements issued by Bangla Desh leaders in exile. For example, a delegate to the International Conference on Bangla Desh held at New Delhi in early September claimed that the guerillas were taking a monthly toll of 5,000 Pakistani casualties and that the Pakistan government was being forced to spend up to 150 crores per month on the insurgency operations: the actual figures in each case were about one-tenth of these claims.

It must be realised that the insurgency in Bangla Desh was not a "revolutionary war" but a "resistance movement". A revolutionary war has the character and potential to develop from low-key hit-and-run operations to large-scale guerilla offensives and eventually to conventional warfare, to defeat the enemy. A resistance movement—like the *maquis* in France during the Second World War—lacks the political and demographic base necessary for the mobilisation of manpower and resources to convert from clandestine to open warfare.

Although the national motivation in Bangla Desh was almost total, the ranks of the Mukti Bahini were filled not so much from a people's base as by intellectuals, students and the middle classes. It was, as has been previously stated, not a revolutionary but a nationalistic movement—and, therefore, destined to be confined to guerilla operations—hit-and-run raids, ambushes and sabotage.

Resistance operations such as the Mukti Bahini's can only hope to succeed if there is a very large degree of military support from a friendly power—or physical intervention. If the Mukti Bahini were to succeed in liberating Pakistan, it would require all the help that the Indian armed forces could give them—morally, materially and, if the occasion arose, by physical intervention.

The story of the Mukti Bahini is related in the next chapter. The point to be made here is that as far as Indian defence plans were concerned, the immediate priorities were to gear up the armed forces to a state of full war preparedness—and to help build the Mukti Bahini up to a pitch at which it could conduct regular operations.

At that stage the overall strategic plan was to hold a purely defensive posture in the north and west and to prepare for military action in the east according to the directions of the government. All this required considerable preparation—the raising of logistical units, units for airfield protection and the regrouping of forces to conform with the strategic plan.

CHAPTER III

The Mukti Bahini

Someone, we hope, will one day assemble the full story of the Freedom Fighters of Bangla Desh. It will be a stirring saga of heroism, tenacity and intense love of country. Never in the history of man's resistance to a foreign oppressor has there been such total motivation as was displayed by the people of Bangla Desh: and of that motivation was the freedom struggle born. A peace loving, gentle, cultured and naturally docile people, the Bengalis have never taken kindly to mercenary or professional militarism: but in them lurks a core of acute political consciousness which when stirred inspires them to grim resistance. The Mogul recognised it—as did the British: but not the Pakistanis.

The account of the Mukti Bahini given in this chapter is largely a reconstruction from published sources, from meetings with Bangla Desh leaders in exile and occasional government releases. The operations of this force, particularly after the majority of its personnel escaped to border sanctuaries, are necessarily still clouded in secrecy—for obvious reasons. Their endeavours and their successes are legion; their contribution to the eventual campaign of liberation, however, will be fully acknowledged only when the whole story can be told. In the meanwhile, the reconstructed account in the following pages will have to suffice for the present purpose. The author hopes to be forgiven if it fails to accord full justice to that noble body of fighters.

It became obvious soon after the Bangla Desh Liberation Army rose up in arms against the Pakistani forces that whatever political mobilisation Sheikh Mujibur Rehman might have preplanned for his party's programme, there had been little attempt made to co-ordinate or organise a military cadre around which a resistance movement could be formed. This was not altogether surprising, because the majority of the East Bengalis serving in the Pakistani armed forces were by tradition apolitical—not unlike attitudes prevalent among Indian officers and men in the old British days. It is true that a certain degree of disaffection had been created among Bengali personnel because of the inequitable rank structure whereby few Bengalis rose to high command, and the tremendous weightage given to West Pakistanis in the Army's class composition; but even so, before mid-February it would have been difficult for any political organisation to make much headway in trying to establish contacts with Bengali members of the armed forces. The pity is that after the nation-stirring events that followed the Sheikh's Declaration of February 12th, and even more so after March 1st, there still was no attempt to establish a co-ordinated resistance plan with officers of the armed forces. On the contrary, some reports indicate that even where individual officers took the initiative to suggest such a course to the Sheikh, their overtures were politely spurned.

The total number of armed East Bengal personnel in East Bengal before 25th March was about 70,000, composed of approximately 6,000 regulars in the six battalions of East Bengal Regiment located in the eastern wing, about 12–15,000 members of the East Pakistan Rifles (a border security organisation) and about 45–50,000 in the *Razakar* organisation, who were trained as homeguards.

The *Razakars*, the main collaborators with the Pakistanis, were of two categories: the *Mujahids*, who were partly armed with obsolete rifles and guns; and the *Ansaris*, who were armed only with *lathis* and spears. The *Mujahids* were almost wholly composed of Bihari or other non-Bengali Muslims; the *Ansaris* were mainly Biharis but also contained some Bengalis— who of course defected to a man when the uprising started.

The *Mujahids* remained staunch henchmen of the Pakistanis throughout the genocide campaign and during the operations: they were responsible for innumerable acts of savagery and brutality under Pakistan Army's orders and were used on an organised scale to abduct young women for Pak officers and men. The *Ansaris* were not nearly as fanatical and, during the operations, large numbers gave themselves up to the Indian Army.

In addition to these military and para-military forces, there were about 45,000 police in the country. Though not all armed, their great strength lay in the fact that as in the rest of the country their political motivation had, unlike in the armed forces, been built up during the crises of February and March—and they rose in revolt when the Pakistani killings started. It was the police who suffered most in the initial extermination drive which started on 25 March. In Dacca and certain other urban centres, the Pakistanis, who had gauged the high degree of nationalistic feeling in the police force during the heady days following Sheikh Mujibur Rehman's election success, attacked many police posts and murdered their occupants *en masse*.

The first approach made by the Sheikh to establish contact with military personnel was on 19 March, when he got in touch with Colonel Osmany. It was typical that of the three points that Colonel Osmany made in a secret circular to Bengali commanders following the Sheikh's communication, the first was that they must not become "embroiled in politics".

During the period that the Pakistani command was building up its strength in the eastern wing, deploying forces and stocking up for its gruesome campaign of terror, every effort was made to render Bengali personnel of the Army ineffective. Key officers were sent out of their units and headquarters on purposeless missions; personnel were disarmed on flimsy pretexts; and, in certain cases, collective murder plans were drawn up by West Pakistani officers to liquidate their Bengali colleagues as soon as the signal was given from Dacca.

Colonel Osmany (who was later appointed Commander-in-

Chief of the Freedom Fighters) has said that Bengali personnel in the army might well have stayed neutral had the Pakistani authorities confined their crack down to selected Bengali politicians. It was the over-kill, the systematic "elitocide" campaign to exterminate professionals, intellectuals and army officers that decided them to revolt.

On 25 March, and in the days immediately following, a number of officers and men were murdered in cold blood. Many senior officers had already been separated from their posts. The result was that when the uprising took place it was mainly under junior leadership—for instance, Major Khaled Musharraf in the Comilla area, Major Zia-ur-Rehman in Chittagong and Major Usman in Chaudanga (near Kushtia).

Zia was an officer of the 8th Battalion of the East Bengal Regiment, stationed in Chittagong. On the morning of 25 March, a few hours before the Pak massacre campaign was scheduled to start, he evaded a trap set by his commanding officer to liquidate him and began to form a group of rebels around him. Eventually, with six officers and about 200 men of the battalion, he took over control of parts of Chittagong. On 27 March he occupied the Radio Station and was able to broadcast his now famous message to the people to take up arms against the Pakistanis.

Although he lost control of the Radio Station on 30 March, he continued to offer resistance in the Chittagong area till mid-April, after which he took his group northwards to the India—Mymensingh border.

The Amrita Bazar Patrika of Calcutta carried a story of the attempt by the Pakistanis to "deport" a large contingent of east Bengal Regiment personnel by sea from Chittagong on the eve of the crack down. However, the Bengalis mutinied, "sea-jacked" the ship they had sailed in and forced the captain to put back to port.

In various centres all over Bangla Desh, army and police personnel rallied round young officers—and within a few days a rebel army of about 10,000 trained men were fighting the Pakistanis in small groups—in the Rangpur-Dinajpur salient in the north, the Rajshahi-Kushtia-Jessore sector facing West Bengal, in the Sylhet and Mymensingh districts, in the key Dacca-Comilla sector and in Chittagong in the extreme south-east. The most organised groups were in the Chittagong and Comilla areas mainly because battalions of the East Bengal Regiment (EBR) had been located in those areas.

The remarkable thing about the spontaneous uprising in Bangla Desh was the effectiveness with which sabotage operations were carried out. Road and rail communications were disrupted, bridges blown up and rivercraft sunk. For a people who had never planned an uprising such as this, the perspicacity and resourcefulness in hitting where it would hurt most amounted to genius: the Pakistanis certainly had not expected sabotage on such a widespread scale.

Major Khaled Musharraf had been a staff officer in a formation headquarters. Shortly prior to 25 March, he had been sent away on patrol on a flimsy pretext—but having become suspicious he began to form a small group around him. He outwitted the instructions to surrender automatic weapons and formed a plan for guerilla operations. When the Pakistani genocide campaign started his group was able to escape north-wards from Brahmanbaria towards Sylhet and thereafter carried out effective sabotage operations—one of the few instances of pre-planned and systematic blowing of bridges and destruction of roads and railways. It was mainly because of the efforts of this group that Sylhet remained isolated from Comilla and Dacca for a long period, thus greatly helping Major Saifullah, the leader of the freedom fighters in Sylhet, whose guerillas almost succeeded in capturing the Sylhet airfield.

The Mukti Fouj were not so successful in the West and in the North, where there was a larger number of cantonments and a greater deployment of Pakistani troops. In fact, in the Dinajpur-Rangpur area there seems to have been very little local leadership for the formation of effective guerilla groups. This area was, until much later, relatively firmly held by the enemy: this perhaps explains why even during the operations the outposts in this area could hold out for so long.

The only effective underground organisation in the western districts was in the Kushtia-Jessore-Khulna region, where the Mukti Fouj was able to organise an escape channel to convoy political and other leaders to India and to establish an Intelligence centre for the Bangla Desh government when it was set up in Indian territory.

In the early part of April, many Mukti Fouj groups fought against local Pakistani forces, often occupying sections of various towns. Unfortunately these temporary successes were grossly exaggerated, both in the reports that emanated from Bangla Desh and as reflected in our press—with the result that for a while a wave of optimism swept the country. The nature of the unequal struggle that was taking place was not at once appreciated.

The Pakistani forces were entrenched in their cantonments, usually located at a distance from the towns and cities. The guerillas succeeded in some instances, Kushtia for one, in occupying a section of the city—claiming liberation successes. Inevitably, when the Pakistani forces rallied forth in strength from their cantonment keeps, the Mukti Fouj suffered losses in the ensuing pitched battles. The Pakistanis suffered losses too, but the odds were heavily against the insurgents. By the third week in April the occupation forces had regained control over most of the towns and cities—and the Mukti Fouj had to go underground to lick its wounds.

It should not be thought that the EBR, the EPR and the police were the only groups who formed the Mukti Fouj. A number of other organisations also joined the resistance movement and contributed greatly. The communists, for example, played a not inconsiderable part in the struggle— particularly in the area immediately north of Dacca.

The communists were split into two parts—the Toha group of Peking-oriented extremists, located mainly in the forest areas north-west of the capital and in the estuarine regions of Noakhali district. The Moscow-oriented Maulana Bhashani communists were both ubiquitous and greater in numbers. Neither group had access to weapons or explosives except perhaps through underground communist channels from across the border.

One of the strongest and most effective local guerilla groups was located in the Tangail area, where a young Bengali revolutionary named Abdel Kader Siddiqi, a dashing, flamboyant and fearless leader (later self-styled "General" and nick-named "the Tiger") formed an effective band of insurgents. The strength of this group eventually grew to 16,000 armed men. It not only dominated the Tangail area, certain areas of Mymensingh District and Dacca, but also played a crucial role in the Indian Army's plans for the liberation of Dacca.

The Mukti Fouj was eventually able to accelerate the organisation of *gram parishads,* village insurgency cells, throughout the country. Although very few of these *gram parishads* were able to take an active part in the insurgency operations, their degree of motivation was so great that they eventually formed a sanctuary in the rural areas from which the guerilla movement could operate. Unlike other resistance movements in history, the Bengali resistance was never so terrorised as to resort to betrayal and treachery.

After the end of April, the Mukti Fouj operations abated considerably—and the next phase started, the long process for the recruitment, organisation, training and equipping of what eventually came to be called the Mukti Bahini.

The sanctuaries sought by the freedom fighters when they went into hiding were strung out along the whole length of the Indo-Bangla border. They established camps, recruited large numbers of educated youth—mainly Muslim but including many Hindus—who escaped from the campaign of "elitocide" let loose on 25 March. They were organised, trained and armed at these camps, and given operational experience. Since most of the recruits were educated youths from schools and colleges, they were easy to train. The normal recruit's training period could be considerably shortened. Every six weeks 2,000 guerillas were being turned out for operational duty. The Mukti Bahini is in fact one of the most highly educated armed forces ever.

At the beginning the guerillas were armed mainly with rifles and submachine guns. As their operations intensified—and they began to score successes against isolated garrisons and patrols of the enemy—their armoury also expanded. By the end of September, many guerilla groups had acquired light machine guns, hand grenades and even mortars. Clandestine factories were set up in the sanctuary areas for the manufacture of such items as anti-personnel and anti-tank mines, booby trap explosives and grenades—albeit of crude and cumbersome design. But they were effective: they began to take their toll of Pakistani lives. Bridges could be blown up, vehicle columns destroyed and, occasionally, even the tracks of enemy tanks damaged.

Reports from the front during the liberation campaign gave ample indications that the re-arming programme for the Bahini was not confined to guerilla groups. It is likely that towards the latter part of this period some of the former regular personnel of the EBR were grouped into regular units or sub-units in order to enable them to operate alongside Indian Army troops should the need arise, particularly in the eastern sector. Besides, the leaders of the Mukti Bahini must have realised that when Bangla Desh was eventually liberated, the administration would feel the need for a cadre of regular troops—for internal security roles to begin with and, subsequently, to form the nucleus of a Bangla Desh Army.

The designation of the force was changed from Mukti Fouj to Mukti Bahini after it changed character from a solely land force to an all-Services organisation. There was a large number of Bengalis among the key personnel of the Pakistan Air Force and Navy. All those located in Bangla Desh at the time of the uprising joined the Fouj: many who were stationed in Pakistan also defected and succeeded in slipping across the border to India. Among them were pilots, highly qualified technicians and specialist personnel. These were quickly absorbed into the freedom movement—and were responsible for expanding the scope of guerilla operations to include river-borne patrolling, frogmen operations and eventually estuarine operations against shipping. In August a number of supply ships were sunk by frogmen operating in Chalna and Chittagong harbours, using limpet mines. In September two British vessels, the 16,000-ton tanker *Teviot* and the 10,000-ton freighter *Chakdina* were severely damaged—a remarkable feat for saboteurs operating so far from base. A number of other vessels were also sunk or damaged in Chalna and Chittagong. On 12 October, the most daring exploit of all took place. By all accounts a Mukti Bahini gun-boat ventured out to the open seas and attacked a British cargo boat, the 7,000-ton *City of St Albans*—peppering its hull and forcing it to limp back to Calcutta. Pakistani waters were thereafter a danger zone for shipping supplying the occupation government and armed forces.

Until July, raids by the guerillas were conducted on a restricted scale—small groups operating 5–10 miles within the Bangla Desh border. Towards the end of the month operations were stepped up: larger groups, often in company strength, were sent out and they penetrated deep into enemy-held territory— even to the extent of fighting pitched battles whenever circumstances were favourable. At Belonia, for instance, 450 Pakistani troops were killed in a battle in which the Bahini lost 70 dead. Eventually, the enemy had to deploy a whole brigade to clear the area. Again near Satkhira the Pakistanis lost 300 soldiers against guerilla losses of about 20. Similarly a number of other well guarded targets were attacked. Over a hundred important road and rail bridges and nearly a thousand minor bridges and culverts were blown up.

Not only was the Pakistani regular army built up to about forty battalions, the best part of four and a half divisions (though not with full complements of armour and artillery) but there was large scale induction of Pakistan Special Forces —a grotesque body of men. Their leaders had been trained by the Americans, but the "Green Berets" of the Pakistan Army were only a parody of their American counterparts; clumsy and unimaginative in operation, they excelled only in committing atrocities.

The Mukti Bahini's aim at this stage was two-fold. Firstly,

to intensify economic warfare; and secondly, to kill Pakistani soldiers and capture their weapons. In both tasks the Bengali guerillas succeeded beyond all expectations. The flourishing tea industry of East Bengal was brought to a halt; large quantities of arms and equipment were captured; and in many areas the Pakistani forces were terrorised into confining their movements to daylight hours.

It was not only the Mukti Bahini operating from the border areas who were responsible for these successes. There were many centres of resistance in the heart of Bangla Desh which were gradually forcing the enemy into a demoralising, defensive attitude. Bands of guerillas in the Dacca area in the narrow corridor between Noakhali and Chittagong, in Sylhet and in a number of other places were gradually eroding the Pakistan Army's domination and control.

The following account compiled from reports of observers, who had visited Mukti Bahini camps inside Bangla Desh and seen things for themselves, gives an indication of the Bahini's capacity and potential at the end of October:

The Indian lieutenant passed the journalists on to a wizened man of perhaps 60 who carried an old carbine, identified himself as "Mukti Bahini"—the guerrilla military arm—and then set off at a brisk pace through a drenching rainstorm. Floundering in the thick mud, the journalists followed him on a twisting four-mile hike through rice paddies and beside a border marker dividing India and East Pakistan. At the end of the march was an abandoned school-house, now identified by a banner as sub-sector headquarters for the "Liberation Forces of Bangla Desh".

Major Najmul Huda, a 33-year-old precisely spoken man who said he had been a Captain in the Pakistani Army, asserted that from the school-house he controls an area of 150 square miles. He has a company of about a hundred regular soldiers who defected to the rebel cause and 7,000 villagers trained by his forces. The guerrillas claim to have implanted such headquarters throughout East Pakistan, and say they are intensifying an insurgency that will drive the regular Pakistani Army from the territory in a year or so.

It is impossible to judge the validity of their claims on a quick hike. But impartial analysts credit the guerrilla organisation with having expanded within seven months from zero to a force of 80,000 to 100,000 men, a figure, roughly equal to the number of regular Pakistani soldiers deployed against them. These analysts feel that the Mukti Bahini may be developing from a rag-tag, hurriedly thrown together force into something of an organisation with increasing capability for coordinated actions.

Authoritative reports circulating in the diplomatic community in East Bengal also support Major Huda's assertion that the Mukti Bahini has "become more aggressive and effective within recent weeks". In the past 20 days, rebel attacks concentrated on communications and logistic lines show a pattern of increasing sophistication in the guerrillas' arms supplies and training, according to these reports, which add to the speculation that India may have recently stepped up tactical support for the guerrillas. They have been helped by the dispersal of Pakistani troops around the frontier over the past two weeks.

The guerrillas' success in the interior has apparently led to increasing retaliation by Pakistani forces against Indian border areas suspected of harbouring them. There are daily reports of shellings of villages and in a few cases Indian areas are said to have been strafed by Pakistani aircraft.

Borya is in an area that was shelled last week. All indications are that the Indian troops camped there have not crossed into East Pakistan to help the guerrillas. Whether they support them in other ways is a matter of bitter dispute. While the Indians deny that they do, Pakistan as a matter of routine describes the guerrillas as Indian agents or puppets.

Major Huda denied that his men receive arms or training from the Indians. He attributed what he described as a significant increase in the number of weapons available to his men in the past few weeks to the increased capture of rifles distributed by the Pakistani Army to loyal civilians.

But there are persistent reports that a major influx of new arms began coming into the Indian border areas about 10 days ago. According to one version, which cannot be confirmed, Indian arms deliveries to the guerrillas were stepped up after the Soviet Union assured India that it would replace Soviet weapons sent on to the rebel forces.

Wounded guerrillas are sent across the border into India for medical care, and the villagers in his area receive food from the Indian Red Cross and from *Oxfam*, Major Huda said.

The guerrillas and the Indian military also undoubtedly exchange intelligence. Observers feel that official leaks in New Delhi to the Indian press, confirmed by reliable Indian sources, show a detailed knowledge on the Indian side of the positioning of Pakistani forces throughout the country.

The apparent growing cohesion within the Mukti Bahini and the emergence of officers like Major Huda as *de facto* district administrators are trends that are being carefully scrutinised by Western observers.

"Some of us assume that East Pakistan will in fact be an independent country at some point", said one Western diplomat. "We don't know if it will take six months or six years. But if it does happen there will be a new generation of leaders who have been formed in the guerrilla battle, and it will be important to know what they are". (*Washington Post* and *The Guardian* (London), 3 November)*.

News Review on Pakistan—Nov. 1971—Institute of Defence Studies and Analyses, New Delhi.

CHAPTER IV

A Positive Posture on the Eastern Front

The hot sweltering months of summer passed by while millions fleeing Pakistani brutality came pouring over the border into Indian refugee camps. By the beginning of August the figure had risen to six millions—and indications were that Pakistan's continuing campaign of terror, coupled with the food shortages that would inevitably follow in the wake of widespread disruption of Bangla Desh agronomy, would push the figures up to ten, twelve, even fifteen millions by the time the winter was over.

It was incumbent on India during this period to maintain a low profile for a sufficient time to achieve three specific aims: diplomatic neutralisation of the Chinese threat; completion of the re-grouping and the raising programmes of the armed forces; and the training of the Mukti Bahini up to a level of operational readiness.

India's Prime Minister, however, had not followed an entirely passive policy. Like her father before her, she seems to possess an ingrained understanding of the nuances of conflict-control as an ingredient of contemporary concepts of strategic confrontation. Even as early as the first week of April—when the armed forces were in a state of imbalance and hesitant to contribute to a policy of escalation that might lead to all-out war, she had taken action to assume a positive military posture along the Bangla Desh border—albeit at a low level of confrontation. She had alerted the Border Security Forces (BSF) of the Home Ministry to handle the situation on the border—where elements of the Mukti Fouj, particularly the EBR and the EPR, were crossing into Indian territory to escape pursuing Pakistani forces. It was the BSF who were the first to receive, accommodate, train and equip the force that was eventually to burgeon out into the Mukti Bahini of Bangla Desh: and it was Mrs Gandhi who saw, more clearly than most of her advisers, that the security threat posed by Pakistan's rampage in Bangla Desh had to be met, from the very beginning, by a degree of military action.

In the traditional concept of international policy-making, recourse is taken to the use of armed force after diplomatic policy fails to maintain peace (or decides that armed action is at last necessary to resolve a diplomatic crisis). Thereafter, the military takes over—to pursue a win-the-war aim. The dichotomy is clear-cut: civilian authorities conduct policies and diplomacy: the military conducts war to victory without civilian participation.

Strategic developments since the Second World War introduced a fundamental change in the precepts of mutual military and political exclusion. Because of the inhibitions imposed by nuclear deterrence and the influence of super-power confrontation over regional strategy, there evolved a new concept of strategy—requiring in both peace and war the orchestration with the military of other instruments of statecraft—political, economic and sociological. In this new concept, military action was shorn of its all-or-nothing characteristic—the use of maximum force to attain decision. Instead, under the new concept, employment, or the threat of employment, of force could be controlled, at a lower level of confrontation, primarily to convey a diplomatic message: and from there, by skilful handling of conflict-control, a strategic dialogue could stretch out the narrow gap between peace and war.

Although for India the more positive and productive step at that stage would have been a partial mobilisation on the western front (which might have prevented large-scale reinforcement of Pakistan's Army in the east) Mrs Gandhi—presumably fearing that such a step might lead quickly to a degree of escalation for which the armed forces were unprepared—chose to act on a lower key in the east. She left the border confrontation to the BSF—who could fulfil the desired role but would be unlikely to excite violent Pakistani military reaction.

As regards the neutralisation of the Chinese threat, a series of developments in Sino-Indian relations during the months that followed could be taken as indications that the Chinese would not actually threaten physical intervention over the Bangla Desh issue. Although on 11 April China had come out with a statement firmly supporting the Pak military junta against the Bangla Desh movement and later followed this up with anti-Indian pronouncements—accusing India of being "reactionary" and "expansionist"—the tone was always moralistic rather than physically threatening. The difference between the threats of 1962 and 1965 and the general behavioral pattern of the Chinese Communist government in 1971 was reassuring. That this was a justifiable appreciation of Chinese intentions was further confirmed when, in November, Yahya Khan sent a high-powered delegation to Peking under Mr Bhutto. The absence of a joint communique at the end of the visit indicated that the mission had been a failure—that the outcome had fallen short of what either Mr Bhutto or President Yahya Khan had expected.

One of the reasons for this reluctance on the part of the Chinese to be drawn into a military involvement in case of an Indo-Pak war was that China was making her debut in the international forum—a process that carries its own built-in restraint. While there had been tentative approaches towards rapprochement between Indian and Chinese envoys, American overtures to China resulting in the world-startling Kissinger visit to Peking and culminating in Communist China's admission to the United Nations as the sole representative of the Chinese people greatly abetted the issue. Within the United Nations China could less confidently afford a strident, rigid and irresponsible line; working within the community of nations, she was less likely to make a unilateral move against India.

Nor were political circumstances the only reasons for China's reluctance to commit herself to military intervention in support of her ally. Ever since 1963, her armies in the north had become locked in a massive military confrontation with the Russians in the boundary dispute along the Usuri River, a confrontation that had already erupted in open conflict. Two years of negotiations had still not produced a resolution of the dispute—and the confrontation continued. With more than half a million troops thus tied up in the north it was unlikely that the Chinese could afford to open a war front on the distant Tibetan border with India.

India's intent in the Indo-Soviet treaty signed in early August was (despite the critical and somewhat nervous reaction it provoked in the west and in some circles in India itself) more in the nature of a surety than the forging of a coalition or bloc. The signatories to the treaty neither envisaged nor implied super-power intervention in the event of an armed conflict between India and Pakistan. One (surely not unintentional) by-product of the treaty was the further neutralisation of the Chinese threat—though the common Sino-American front that devolved during the active Indo-Pakistan hostilities (despite the fact that their coincidental interests were for widely divergent reasons) was unforeseen.

The armed forces spent the intervening months in feverish preparation to meet the threat of all-out war against Pakistan. The Army, particularly, had a Herculean task—the raising and re-grouping of forces to meet a three-front confrontation. Top priority in General Manekshaw's list of preparatory requirements would have to be the re-grouping of his forces and material resources in order to make Eastern Command operationally capable of conducting a war in Bangla Desh should Pakistan decide to open hostilities in the West.

Until then Eastern Command had been a formation geared almost solely for mountain operations in the northern and the north-eastern sectors. Except for one infantry division earmarked for the defence of the West Bengal-East Bengal border opposite Calcutta, the rest of its forces were oriented either for the Himalayan borders (an army corps in Sikkim and an army corps in NEFA) or for internal security in Nagaland and in the Mizo Hills. The divisions deployed for these roles were all mountain divisions. They contained no bridging or other river crossing equipment, which would be required in large quantities for operations in Bangla Desh. Their artillery was mainly pack or towed mountain artillery, too light to be effective against the concrete pill-boxes and fortified bunkers that would face them in Pakistan-held territory in Bangla Desh. There was very little armour. Last but not least, the transport requirements for logistical support of operations in the riverine terrain of Bangla Desh would have to be found from elsewhere —Eastern Command possessed only an insignificant fraction of the resources required for this kind of operation.

Even the inter-Services command system had been oriented towards operations in the Himalayas. While the Army's Eastern Command was at Calcutta, Eastern Air Command was at Shillong, with responsibility for operations in the north— not over Bangla Desh. There was no co-ordination link with the Navy. If there was to be a war in Bangla Desh, the inter-Services joint command system would have to be radically altered.

The Army Chief accepted the risk of diverting some of his reserve mountain divisions facing the north to provide forces necessary in Eastern Command. He sent two divisions to bolster up the West Bengal-East Bengal border and ordered the raising of a new Corps Headquarters (II Corps) for command and control of these divisions under Eastern Army.

The Nagaland division and the division operating in the Mizo Hills were extricated from their commitment and made available for the Bangla Desh operation, grouped under a Corps Headquarters loaned from the northern front (IV Corps).

A regiment of medium armour and two regiments of light tanks (*PT-76* Russian amphibians) were diverted to Eastern Command. The biggest problem, however, was artillery support

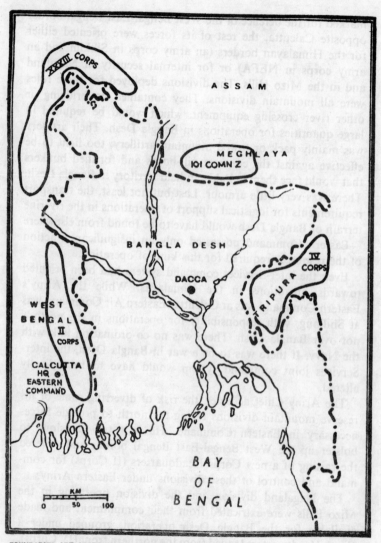

BOUNDARIES ARE APPROXIMATE AND NOT TO SCALE

Build-up for Eastern Command

—and artillery would be a crucial factor against an enemy whose infantry was armed with more than twice the number of light and heavy automatic weapons. (The two divisions from Nagaland and the Mizo Hills possessed no artillery whatsoever).

By denuding other fronts, Army Headquarters was able to make up most of the medium and field artillery deficiencies. In the event, as Pakistani officers have since confirmed, the artillery arm of the Indian Army played a crucial role in the operations.

Bridging resources were built up almost from scratch to an extent that Eastern Army could (and did) lay 10,000 feet of bridging at any given moment—the largest bridging effort in military history.

The inter-Services joint command system was reorganised to ensure the highest degree of co-ordination. To Headquarters Eastern Command was sent an Advance Headquarters of Eastern Air Command, under an Air Commodore, and an Indian Naval Headquarters representing the Flag Officer-in-Chief, Eastern Naval Command at Visakhapatnam. The foresight displayed in effecting this joint command organisation paid full dividends when war eventually broke out. Unlike in other wars, the Indian land forces operating in Bangla Desh were not deprived of close air support while the Air Force fought its own battles in the air. Eastern Air Command's liaison cell at Eastern Command was able to ensure that a certain number of sorties in support of ground troops was always available—no matter what the air war situation. The inter-Services joint command system made it possible not only to obtain naval gun and Fleet Air Arm support to the Army but also to mount at least one combined operation at short notice to fulfil the Army Commander's aim.

The planning, staff work and management required to complete this re-grouping and reorganisation programme was a test of the maturity and professional skill in all the Services and at all levels. And the Services passed the test with flying colours—as coming events were amply to prove.

By the beginning of November, the forces for the Bangla Desh operation had been built up to three Army Corps with a total of about seven divisions. The Air Force had activated Kumbigram airfield and were complete in their requirements of interceptor fighter squadrons, fighter-bombers and transport squadrons. The Eastern Fleet of the Navy was at war readiness. The most arduous task had been to build up the operational infrastructure on the eastern front—in Silchar and Tripura—including the widening and black-topping of roads (all undertaken under monsoon conditions).

Should Yahya Khan declare war in the west, or Niazi carry out his blustering threat to escalate the confrontation by invading Indian territory, Eastern Command would be ready for the task in hand.

By mid-summer, the Indian Army had begun to assume border responsibilities in the eastern border—the next step in the "dialogue" with Pakistan. It largely relieved the BSF of the task of liaising with the Mukti Bahini, though the latter continued to offer material assistance to the guerillas.

Pakistan's reaction to Mukti Bahini activity along the Indian border was greater escalation—by pushing forces up to the border—in the process sending further waves of refugees lapping over the border into India. At the same time, the Pakistani Army in the west feverishly built defences along the Cease-Fire line in J & K State and along the border between East and West Punjab. The months of September and October were spent in constructing pill-boxes, bunkers and observation towers—and the laying of extensive minefields. By 12 October, of the 3,00,000 or more troops in the western wing, more than 80 per cent were in forward positions—in some places only a few hundred yards from the Indian border.

On the eastern borders they went even further—particularly on the Tripura front, where they crossed the international border in several places—for example at Andermanik, Baganbasar and Hinsiku—and even dug defensive positions on the Indian side.

By this time, the Mukti Bahini's guerilla offensive against

Pakistani troops—both in the border regions and in the interior—had been stepped up and their achievements had reached significant proportions. In most cantonments, including Dacca, troops were having to confine their movements to daylight hours—seldom venturing out into the countryside except in large columns. This, together with large-scale sabotage activities was beginning seriously to disrupt the occupation government's administrative control in the country. From the border sanctuaries more ambitious operations were undertaken—company strong bands of guerillas mounting hit-and-run raids on isolated detachments of Pakistani troops, ambushes to waylay vehicle columns and patrols.

Towards the end of October, Mukti Bahini guerillas began to claim "liberation" of strips of territory—both adjacent to the Indian border and in the interior—in Mymensingh, Dinajpur, Rangpur, Rajshashi, Kushtia, Jessore, Khulna and Noakhali districts. In some of these "liberated" areas the Bangla Desh government-in-exile sent in administrators to reorganise the administration at village and union levels.

Unable to strike back against the evanescent bands of Bahini guerillas, the Pakistani high command decided to take reprisals against India. They began to shell encampments on Indian territory, raid and set fire to Indian villages, kidnap village leaders and carry out sabotage activities such as blowing up bridges and railway tracks—particularly in the Nadia district of West Bengal and in Cooch Behar and West Dinajpur, in the Karimganj area of Assam, in Meghalaya and in Tripura. On 23 October, the Chief Minister of Assam reported that a large band of *razakars* had crossed over into Goalpara District (west of Gauhati)—but later surrendered to Indian authorities.

Lieut-General Niazi, Commander of the Pakistani forces and Military Governor of Bangla Desh, is reported to have sought and obtained permission to enter Indian territory in pursuit of Mukti Bahini guerillas. Speaking at a gathering in Saidpur in the third week of October, he declared that "war would be fought on Indian territory."

As Pakistan's trans-border operations grew in intensity, it was inevitable that the Pakistani Army would clash with Indian forces. The first such major incident occurred at Kamalpur (Tripura) at the end of October.

Kamalpur, a village eight kilometres within the Indian border, was alleged by Pakistan to be a Mukti Bahini camp. Continuous shelling by Pak artillery had resulted in a number of casualties among civilians: on 20 and 22 October, the shelling killed a total of 22 civilians and wounded over 90. Compelled to take defensive measures, the BSF and Mukti Bahini, with support from the Indian Army, took steps to silence the Pakistani guns and destroy their positions in Dhulia tea estate. In this operation, a battalion of the re-raised EBR took a prominent part.

In November, there were a number of air violations over Indian territory both in J&K in the west and in Tripura—presumably on reconnaissance missions.

The next positive step towards escalation was taken by Pakistani forces at Boyra, near Ranaghat in West Bengal.

Boyra is a village on the Indian side of the border, on the route that links Calcutta to Jessore, one of the three major cantonments in Bangla Desh—also containing one of the three airports in the country from which *Sabre* jets could operate. For tactical as well as emotional reasons, Jessore was a special target for the Mukti Bahini—it was here that they had suffered one of their major defeats in pitched battle during the early days of the insurgency. The Mukti Bahini had established a major base in Bangla Desh territory adjacent to Boyra.

On 21 November, Pakistani troops supported by tanks and artillery launched an offensive against the "liberated" territory around Boyra, which itself came under heavy shelling and where Indian troops suffered casualties. The Indian Army mounted a local counter-attack, destroying 13 Pakistani *Chaffee* tanks and threw the Pakistanis back. It was at this battle that three intruding *Sabre* jets were brought down by a flight of IAF *Gnats*—and two of the pilots captured as they parachuted down on Indian territory.

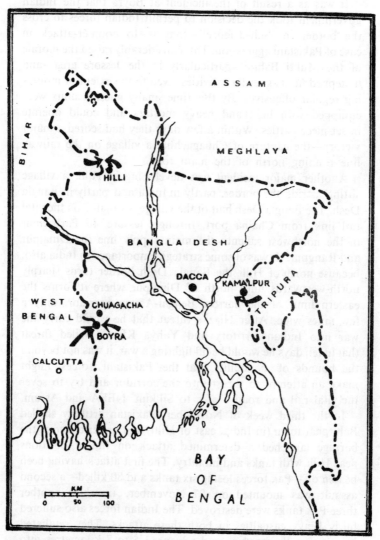

BOUNDARIES ARE APPROXIMATE AND NOT TO SCALE

The Escalating Battles, October-November

It was as a result of the incident at Boyra that the Indian government took the decision to permit Indian forces to cross the border in "self-defence"—that is, to counter-attack in case of Pakistani aggression. This considerably raised the morale of the Mukti Bahini—particularly in the Jessore area—and it stepped up its guerilla activities, even to the extent of mounting regular offensives. By this time, many guerilla units were equipped with light and heavy mortars and could operate in set-piece battles. Within a few days they had scored a major victory—the capture of Chuagachha, a village on the railway line running north of the main road.

Another major incident was developing in Hilli, a village sitting astride the border, partly in India and partly in Bangla Desh. The Bangla Desh half of the village is situated on the vital rail link from Chalna port, through Jessore, to Parbatipur in the northwest salient—the main supply line for Dinajpur and Rangpur. It was of some strategic importance to India also, because north of Hilli the Bangla Desh border turns sharply north-westwards until north of Dinajpur where it forms the eastern limit of the narrow Bengal-Assam corridor, only a few miles wide. After Niazi's threat that he would carry the war into Indian territory and Yahya Khan's veiled threat that in ten days he would be off fighting a war, it was not beyond the bounds of possibility that the Pakistani forces might make an attempt to thrust into the corridor and try to sever the' vital rail and road l of c to Sikkim, NEFA and Assam.

In the third week of November, Pakistan artillery shelled Balurghat town (in India, east of Hilli) and under cover of the barrage launched a determined attack on Indian positions near Hilli with tanks and infantry. The first attack having been beaten off—Pak forces losing six tanks and 80 killed—a second assault was mounted on 27 November, in which another three Pak tanks were destroyed. The Indian forces also suffered fairly heavy casualties in both these attacks. They retaliated by crossing the border—and advanced 5 to 7 kilometres into Bangla Desh.

This battle, which lasted three days, constituted the heaviest fighting to date: it was obvious that Pakistan was determined to escalate the scale of operations. Soon after the Hilli battle, the PAF further escalated the operations by a blatant fighter-bomber attack on Agartala airfield—while their propaganda machine accused India (for the second time in a fortnight) of launching "a massive attack on seven fronts". (The first time they had mentioned an attack by 12 Indian divisions.)

India was not unprepared for an offensive—should that be what the Pakistan government wished to provoke. Mrs Gandhi had made one last attempt, during her visit to western capitals, to persuade the governments of the United States, Britain, France, West Germany and others to prevail upon Yahya Khan to negotiate a settlement with Sheikh Mujibur Rehman. At the same time, she was firm in her resolve that the military "dialogue" would be pursued from a position of strength and positive stance. She would deny the Indian forces the strategic liberty of aiming for an operational objective in Bangla Desh: but she would not hamstring their tactical options to retaliate against aggression. And if the escalation were pushed to the point of war, she would give them the all clear they awaited.

CHAPTER V

Pakistan Attacks in the West

Despite the fact that the confrontation on the eastern front was gradually mounting in intensity, there was no indication that India would invade Bangla Desh. The policy announced by the Prime Minister that Indian troops would cross the border only in "self-defence" implicitly imposed limits on the degree of penetration. This might possibly extend to 10–15 miles, that is, about the range at which forward bases for enemy raids and attacks could be set up: but it could go no further without definitely effecting a change of policy to one of open aggression—and this step the Indian government was not yet prepared to take.

Although President Yahya Khan had said on 25 November that in ten days he "might not be here in Rawalpindi... (but) off fighting a war", this was taken more as an attempt at bravdo than as a serious indication of aggressive intent. There was little he could gain from an all-out war against India, to which the conflict would inevitably escalate. So long as there was no actual war between the two countries, Pakistan's isolated eastern army could somehow hope to hold out in Bangla Desh—because it would be many months before the Mukti Bahini could, by itself, pose a serious threat. It might, with trans-border support from the Indian Army, succeed in liberating certain territories around the periphery of the state, even extensive enough to enable the Bangla Desh government in exile to move in; but it was beyond their capability to capture any of the Pakistani cantonment strongholds. And so long as Pakistan preserved a military presence in the greater part of the state, there was no danger of international recognition of Bangla Desh. On the other hand, should the situation on the western front escalate to a state of war, India would be given just the opportunity she sought to embark on a liberation campaign in Bangla Desh in support of the Mukti Bahini. From the Pakistani view-point, therefore, it was imperative to avoid escalation.

Why then did Yahya Khan launch an attack in the west? The answer perhaps lies in the self-delusion that he, like others among his colleagues, has indulged for so long. The Pakistani high command has for a number of years nursed a pipedream about launching a massive, surprise offensive deep into Indian territory—spearheaded by armoured formations, *a la* Moshe Dayan. Unfortunately for them, Hamid Khan (Pakistan Army Chief of Staff) is not a Dayan; nor are Pakistanis Israelis: besides, India is not a restricted piece of territory like the Sinai desert in which a thrust such as the above could, even if successful, prove instantly decisive.

By the end of November the Pakistani high command must have realised that the Indian Army had deployed in full strength on the west, its infantry divisions backed up by a number of armoured brigades—besides the formidable 1st Armoured Division. As for its own forces, the two divisions that Pakistan had begun to raise in May to replace the divisions sent to the eastern wing were still below strength and not fully operational. No one but an incurable optimist would, in those circumstances, hope for the cherished breakthrough to materialise. And yet that is exactly what they attempted—and with incredible ineptitude.

At 5.45 pm on 3 December, a pre-emptive air-strike was launched on a number of Indian airfields—Srinagar, Avantipur, Pathankot, Uttarlai, Jodhpur, Ambala and Agra. Later that night, which was a night of full moon, a second wave of aircraft came over to deliver a repeat blow. Incredible as it may seem, these attempts were so clumsy that not one Indian aircraft was lost on the ground: the "Israeli-type" pre-emptive attack was a total failure. Not only that; within 24 hours

the back of the Pakistani Air Force (PAF) had been broken
by the Indian Air Force (IAF) counter-strike.

The PAF plan seems to have been to make a preliminary
strike at last light to damage the runways of the airfields so
that the parked aircraft would be unable to take off; the second
and subsequent strikes were supposed to finish them off.
The PAF assumed, firstly that most of our squadrons had been
sent up to the forward airfields; and, secondly, that they would
be parked in the open.

Although all the forward airfields had been made operational,
dispersion of aircraft was planned in great detail. In any case,
most of the planes were ensconced in concrete pens—where
only a direct hit could do any damage. There must have been
a drastic break-down of Pak Intelligence for them to have
expected to put our airforce out of action, especially as the
raids were carried out on very minor scale—two or three
aircraft attacking each airfield. Such a timid attempt never
had a chance of success.

The Indian Air Force went into action later that night and
continued mounting operations in a rising crescendo till they
reached the peak of 500 sorties per day—the highest air effort
mounted anywhere since the Second World War. The IAF
attacked Chanderi, Shorkot, Sargodha, Muri, Mianwali,
Marur (Karachi), Risalwalla (Rawalpindi) and Changa Manga
(Lahore). Subsequently it was learnt that over 25 aircraft
were hit. There must have been serious damage to radar
installations and runways because after the first abortive
series of strikes the PAF ceased to be a serious air threat. By
the evening of 4 December, the IAF had established air
superiority.

Pakistani propaganda that the PAF raids were in retaliation
against multi-pronged Indian land offensives all along the
Punjab-Rajasthan borders convinced no one. Mr Murray
Sayles, correspondent of the *Sunday Times* (London) who
was in Peshawar on 2 December, wrote:

It was clear that the decision (to launch an attack) had been taken when, on Thursday December 2, the 7th Division stationed in Peshawar, moved forward to the front under cover of darkness. Any defensive strategy would keep the reserve in hand until the direction of the main attack from the other side had been identified. The move of the 7th Division meant that Pakistan had decided to attack first.

As Mr Sayles reports, the first Pakistani attack went in at 8.30 pm on 3 December, against the Indian Army's Poonch and Chhamb sectors.

Land Forces

Pakistan Army in the west consisted of about ten infantry divisions (two of them newly raised) a few independent brigades, two armoured divisions and an independent armoured brigade. The grouping was as follows:

In the Kashmir sector: 12th Pakistani Occupied Kashmir (POK) Division in the northern sector;

23 POK Division on the Kotli-Poonch front.

In the Sialkot sector: II Pak Corps, with headquarters at Sialkot, consisting of 8, 15 and 17 Infantry Divisions and 6 Armoured Division. The responsibility of this Corps included the Pathankot-Dera Baba Nanak front;

In the Central sector: IV Pak Corps with headquarters at Lahore, consisting of 10 and 11 Infantry Divisions and 8 Independent Armoured Brigade. The responsibility of the Corps included the Lahore-Amritsar axis and the Khem Karan area.

In the Mooltan sector: I Pak Corps with headquarters at Mooltan, consisting of 7 and 33 Infantry Divisions, 25 Infantry Brigade and 1 Armoured Division. The responsibility of this Corps extended south as far as Fort Abbas opposite Anupgarh in Rajasthan.

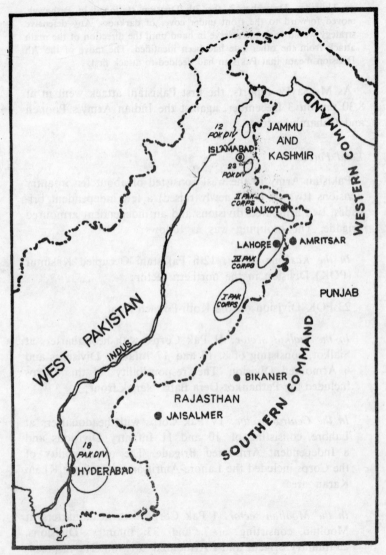

BOUNDARIES ARE APPROXIMATE AND NOT TO SCALE

Pakistani Dispositions in the West

In the Southern sector: 18 Infantry Division and two armoured regiments, with headquarters at Hyderabad (Sind).

From these dispositions, it was appreciated by our high command that the most likely sectors where the Pak army would attempt offensives would be, firstly, on the Sialkot front, with the aim of cutting either the Jammu-Poonch or the Pathankot-Jammu road links to isolate our forces: and secondly, a thrust by I Pak Corps in the southern Punjab. The latter could be the much vaunted "deep Israeli-type thrust".

Indian forces were only marginally superior in overall strength. They were grouped as follows:

Western Command
(Lieutenant-General K.P. Candeth)

General Candeth commanded the bulk of the forces on western front besides holding responsibility for the northern front facing the Chinese—from Ladakh in the north-west to the Himachal Pradesh sector up to the passes north of Simla.

His forces on the western front were grouped in three army corps, besides the Army Headquarters reserve—which was also in his territorial command. The three corps commanders were: Lieut-General Sartaj Singh, Lieut-General N.C. Rawlley and Lieut-General K.K. Singh.

The area of General Candeth's responsibility in the west stretched from J & K state in the north down to the borders of Rajasthan.

Southern Command
(Lieutenant-General G.G. Bewoor)

General Bewoor had moved his advance headquarters up from Poona and was responsible for the Rajasthan front.

As stated earlier, the Pakistani army launched a major

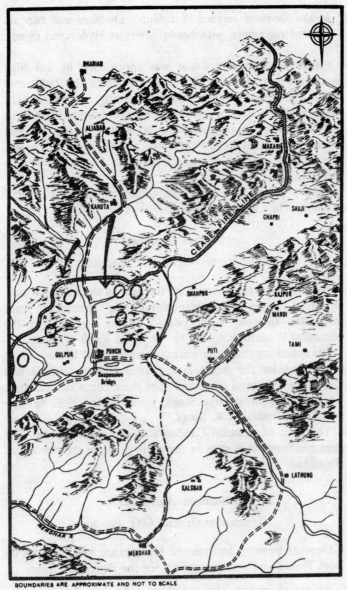

BOUNDARIES ARE APPROXIMATE AND NOT TO SCALE

The Attack on Poonch

offensive in the south-west of Jammu & Kashmir state shortly
after the PAF air strike went in on the evening of 3 December.
If the aim was to capture a piece of Kashmir territory by a
pincer movement, this attack also failed miserably.

In the Poonch sector, an "Azad" Kashmir infantry brigade
launched an attack against Poonch from the direction of
Kahuta in the north-west, while commandos infiltrated behind
the Poonch area to cut the road link. Supported by artillery
barrages, the attack was launched with determination—but
our forces were ready for them. The frontal thrust made little
progress, with the result that it could not effect a link-up
with the commandos. When the Indian Air Force began pounding their troop concentrations in the forests north-west of
Poonch, the enemy decided to call off the attack.

On the night of 9/10 December, the enemy prepared for
a second offensive from the same direction. This time the
IAF strafed and bombed them in their assembly areas—and
the attack fizzled out. It was then the turn of the Poonch
forces to go on to the counter-offensive. A brigade column
moved out towards Hajira, with the aim of dominating the
Poonch-Kotli road. By the 16 December, several posts flank-
ing the road had been occupied by Indian forces.

In the Chhamb sector, the Indian forces were at a slight
disadvantage in that the Munawar Tawi river flows to the east
of Chhamb. The Indian defences, though based on the line
of the Tawi, had covering positions to the west—only 50
miles from the Pak Army's base at Kharian. The Akhnur
"dagger", a Pakistani salient south of Akhnur, threatens the
rear of the defences. It was here, in 1965, that the Pak forces
had scored a major success by driving our troops back to
within a few miles of Akhnur.

The Pak II Corps offensive was led by two infantry brigades and a regiment of mixed Chinese *T-59* and *Sherman*
tanks. Supported by heavy artillery barrages and PAF strafing,
the attack was launched on the evening of 3 December—
simultaneously with the offensive against Poonch. The initial
thrust was held—our forces destroying 6 enemy tanks. On

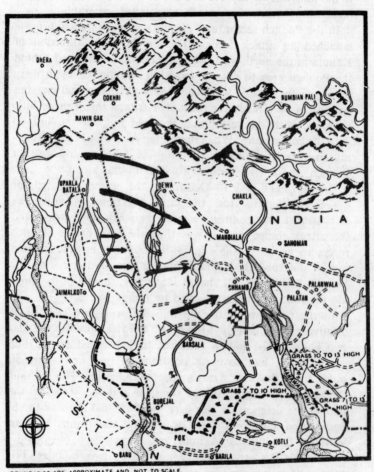

The Attack on Chhamb

December 5, Tikka Khan, the Corps Commander, threw in another brigade into the attack and another regiment of armour. This thrust cost him 23 *T*-59 tanks, much of the killing being done by the IAF. The Indian Army's main defences held the attack but Chhamb, across the Munawar Tawi, had to be abandoned. The withdrawal, however, was carried out well— not a single man or tank being lost in the process.

In the meanwhile, the Indian forces east of Akhnur struck out at the "dagger" salient and cleared the area of enemy— thus safeguarding the rear of the Chhamb garrison.

The enemy, under the crass leadership of Tikka Khan, continued to launch repeated frontal assaults against well-prepared positions, incurring heavy losses. By 10 December, he had committed a full division plus a brigade and three armoured regiments. By then, though the PAF *MIG-19s* and *Sabre Jets* continued to be active (this was the one sector in which the PAF was in evidence) the IAF had gained local superiority and gave close support to the ground troops in full measure. In all these futile attacks, Tikka Khan lost some 3,000 troops and nearly 50 tanks. By 12 December, he had had enough. The "Butcher" of Baluchistan and Dacca lived up to his reputation even as far as his own men were concerned.

In the rest of the J&K theatre, it was the Indian Army that took the initiative—though not with the intention of launching major offensives or acquiring Pakistani-held territory. General Sartaj Singh, the Corps Commander, aimed at "rationalising" the Ceasefire Line—that is offsetting local tactical disadvantages such as removing threats to his l of c, denying the enemy easy routes for infiltration and capturing dominating heights overlooking Indian Army positions. Although these operations had limited aims, the carrying out of the tasks demanded some hard fighting by our troops, because the Pakistanis had, over the years, built very strong defences along the Ceasefire Line.

In the Kargil sector, where the Indian Army's l of c to Leh, via the Zoji La pass, is dominated by heights occupied by Pakistani forces, the "straightening out" of the line entailed the capture of about 15 enemy posts located at heights of 16,000 feet and more. All the attacks were launched at night when, at that season of the year, the ground temperatures sank to below minus 17 degrees centigrade.

In the Tithwal sector, where a large salient of Pak-held territory lies on the east bank of the Kishenganga river and thus poses a threat to the Indian 1 of c from Sopur, the enemy was cleared from the greater part of Lippa Valley, west of Tut Mari Gali pass. Similarly, in the Uri sector, where the Haji Pir salient provides easy infiltration access to Gulmarg, Indian forces captured posts in the Tosh Maidan area to neutralise this threat.

By the time the Ceasefire came, the Corps Commander's aim—to remove local threats—had been almost completely achieved.

In the Jaisalmer sector, an enemy infantry brigade supported by a regiment of armour (mixed *T-59s* and *Shermans*) launched an attack on our positions at Longanewala—probably a spoiling attack in anticipation of a thrust by Indian forces towards the road and rail link at Rahim Yar Khan. It was a bold idea but it had not reckoned with the sands of the desert. The soft vehicles of the supporting troops bogged down first, soon after crossing our border. Then it was the turn of the armour, separated from its supporting column, to flounder in the soft desert, forming an easy target for our aircraft. As one of the IAF *HF-24* pilots described it: "It was like a duck shoot—only we had sitting ducks to shoot at". Sortie after sortie went into the attack and before long more than 20 enemy tanks had been destroyed. The next day a further kill took place, only this time the targets were the long columns of soft vehicles. All in all, the Longanewala battle turned out to be quite a disaster for the enemy.

The only other areas where the Pakistanis made limited gains were in places where small enclaves of Indian territory were located on the far side of rivers or obstacles. Indian forces also quickly occupied Pakistani territory in such tactically unfavourable locations.

Of the three bridges over the rivers Ravi and Sutlej where they form the Indo-Pak boundary, the only one that lay in Indian territory was the Hussainiwalla bridge near Ferozepur: there is a small Indian enclave on the far bank of the river, exposed to Pakistani threat.

On the night of 3/4 December, Pakistani forces launched an attack against this enclave in some strength. Fighting a delaying action, in which the Pakistanis lost 18 tanks, the Indian garrison made a pre-planned withdrawal to the east bank of the river— during which the bridge itself was heavily shelled and damaged by the enemy.

Retaliating in kind, the Corps Commander, General Rawlley, ordered an offensive to capture the Sehjra salient, north-west of Ferozepur. This salient posed a threat not only to Khem Karan but also to the Harike bridge further up the Sut-lej. The attack was to go in on the night of 5/6 December.

The attack came as a complete surprise to the enemy. Indian troops made an approach along the open and sandy river-bed leading to a twenty-foot escarpment behind which the Pak defences were located. It was the one approach the defenders thought the Indians would not take—with the result that Sehjra was soon captured and the threat to Khem Karan and Harike removed.

Similarly, on December 6/7, Indian forces attacked and captured the Pak enclave on the eastern side of the Ravi guarding the Dera Baba Nanak bridge. This enclave was very strongly fortified, the enemy having spent months in constructing pill-boxes and bunkers along the bund, concrete mortar positions and high observation towers. Here again, it was surprise that unbalanced the enemy, the Indian assault coming in from an unexpected flank, after several feints from the direction from which the enemy expected an attack. By the morning of 7 December, the enclave was in Indian hands—and, consequently, the control of the bridge was gained.

In keeping with government's policy and the strategic

plan, the Indian armed forces confined their major operations to the offensive-defensive—that is maintaining the strategic defensive but resorting to local offensive action only to gain a tactical advantage.

A major threat to India's J&K theatre has always been along the southern boundary of the State. Not only the road link to Jammu but also Pathankot base itself lies close to the border. Pakistan's II Corps (Sialkot) the strongest of the Pak Army Corps, could with the greatest of ease either cut the road link or launch an attack on Pathankot itself. It was vital therefore to pinch out the Shakargarh salient that threatens the Pathankot base and to carry out similar operations wherever the tactical disadvantage was reckoned to be crucial. It is with this aim that a major operation (but in limited depth) was undertaken—to capture Shakargarh.

The offensive was launched along three axes—two striking southwards from the general direction of the Kathua-Samba stretch of the main Pathankot-Jammu road; and a third, subsequent thrust from the Gurdaspur area striking westward. The operation started on the night of 5/6 December and lasted till the Ceasefire, culminating in the biggest tank battle of the war.

The country is generally flat: the biggest obstacles to movement are a number of spate nullahs and rivers running north to south—the widest being the Basantar Nullah, which flows to the east of Shakargarh. The two major towns in this salient are Zafarwal, about 15 kilometres south of the Jammu border and 45 kilometres east of the Gurdaspur border, and Shakargarh, situated roughtly between Zafarwal and Gurdaspur.

The two northern thrusts had reached the outskirts of Shakargarh and Nurkot by 8 December—the rate of advance having been slowed down by extensive enemy minefields laid in great depth. The enemy strength in this area was about one infantry brigade supported by a squadron of armour.

The Pakistani forces had been expecting an attack in the Chawinda-Phillaura area (where in 1965, the same I Corps

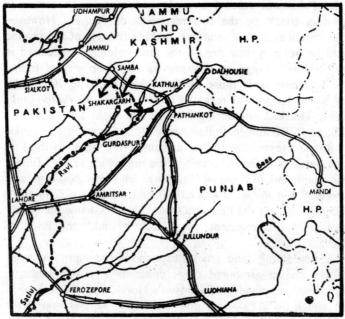

BOUNDRIES ARE APPROXIMATE AND NOT TO SCALE

Indian Offensive at Shakargarh

of the Indian Army had attacked and captured Phillaura
as a preliminary to the attack on Sialkot. The present Corps
Commander, General K.K. Singh, had then commanded
1 Armoured Division of I Corps). However, when Tikka
Khan realised that a concerted effort was being made to capture the Shakargarh salient, he reacted quickly and sent two
armoured regiments (*Pattons*) from 6 Armoured Division to
re-inforce the brigade in Shakargarh.

The Indian attack from the eastern side went in on the night
of 8/9 December, across the River Ravi—supported, as were
the other two, by armour and artillery.

The critical point of the operation was reached when the
western-most column reached the outskirts of Zafarwal.

The Pakistanis reacted strongly and sent in an armoured counter-attack by the two regiments of *Pattons*. However, the Indian Army's *Centurions,* making full use of the ground and by holding their fire till the tank columns had closed in to 900 yards range, quickly proved the superiority of Indian tank-gunners over those of the Pakistanis. The 1965 story of Khem Karan was repeated in this battle—45 *Patton* tanks being knocked out during the day and night long battle on 15 and 16 December. Indian Army's losses were only 15 tanks.

Poona Horse, the Indian armoured regiment involved in this battle, was the same unit as the one which in 1965 (under the command of Colonel Tarapore, who was posthumously awarded the *Param Vir Chakra*) had done so well in the I Corps battle on the Phillaura front. The nick-name the enemy had given this regiment was "Fakhr-i-Hind," the Pride of India.

A fascinating (and true) story about the *esprit de corps* of the Indian armoured corps concerns a young major, a squadron commander, of Hodson's Horse. Ordered to launch an attack on a Pakistani position across the Basantar River which was supported by eight *Patton* tanks (as he saw for himself on a helicopter-borne reconnaissance) he decided on a dawn attack, so that he could negotiate the soggy river-bed during the hours of darkness.

While crossing the river during the night before his D-Day, the poor unfortunate found one after another of his tanks bogging down in the sand. He spent the whole night pulling out his tanks, only to find that as he towed out one another got stuck. Eventually, at 4 am he found himself with only four tanks on the enemy side of the river. Fortunately, he had created enough noise during the night to make the enemy think a whole regiment was crossing over.

In the half-light of dawn, he attacked the enemy tank positions. To his utter consternation, he saw the Pakistani crews abandon their tanks and make for home.

When he had rounded up the prisoners, the young Major was seething—chagrined beyond description. He gathered the Pak crews together and vented his wrath upon them: "Don't you have any *sharm* (shame)? You have let down the armoured corps. You are supposed to stand and fight. You have cut our noses (brought shame upon us)". And with that he marched them off to regimental headquarters.

After the tank battle, the three columns moved forward till they were in contact with the defences of both Zafarwal and Shakargarh. Here again, the Ceasefire came just in time to save the enemy from losing those two towns.

The only sector in which an offensive in any depth was undertaken was in southern command's area of responsibility in Rajasthan. The intention there was to force the enemy to commit his strategic reserve—that is, I Pak Corps, which included Pakistan's I Armoured Division and an infantry division—which still had not been committed. In this aim it entirely succeeded.

The enemy's spoiling attack at Longanewala having failed, General Bewoor, GOC-in-C Southern Command, struck out at two points. From his northern Jaisalmer sector he sent out a column to capture Islamgarh—but the sands in this part of the desert were too treacherous to commit greater forces or to aim for an objective in depth. Further south, along the old Bombay-Sind railway axis, he launched a more determined thrust.

Gadra was taken easily—while along the railway axis a brigade struck out for Khokrapar and beyond. At the same time, a whole series of long-range raiding columns were sent out into the salient between Nagar Parka and the railway axis. Special Forces dominated the area, liquidating Pak outposts—and within a few days the whole salient was under our control. Meanwhile, the column along the railway axis forged ahead and were shortly besieging Naya Chor—which, like Shakargarh, was saved only by the Ceasefire.

The enemy reacted as we had hoped they would. 33 Infantry Division was sent racing down from Pak I Corps to re-inforce the Rahim Yar Khan-Hyderabad sector. There was no longer any question of an enemy capability (if ever there was) of

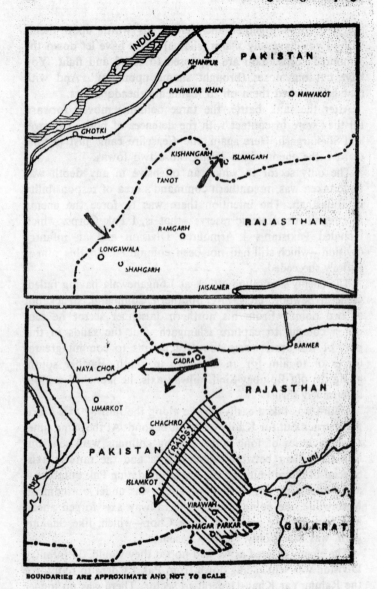

Indian Offensives in Rajasthan

launching a major offensive. The offensive-defensive strategy had paid off. Western and Southern Commands had seen to it that Army Headquarters would be relieved of any anxiety about its Western front and would feel free to pursue the light-ning offensive in Bangla Desh.

CHAPTER VI

The Lightning Concept

From the moment the Indian General Staff began planning for the liberation of Bangla Desh, it became apparent that the key factor in the operation was going to be speed—for both political and military reasons; yet all the circumstances indicated that speed, or mobility, was going to be the most difficult thing to achieve.

It was obvious from the point of view of international complications that Pakistan was banking on support or even intervention of its two super-allies, the United States and China, in case of an Indian attack on Bangla Desh. Yahya Khan made no secret of the fact that he expected to invoke the CENTO or SEATO Treaty to bring the Americans in on his side; and though the Chinese had given no indication that they would physically intervene in case of war, the Pakistani President must have relied on the assumption that if he could hold out for long enough, a combination of military support and diplomatic action by the Chinese would halt India's war of liberation. It was therefore essential for his eastern wing forces to delay the Indian advance for a sufficient period for these two great powers to manoeuvre. Possibly, he had already been given a hint about future "manoeuvres" of the mighty Seventh Fleet.

As with all commanders faced with the task of defending a long coast-line or border Lieut-General Niazi, the Pakistani Commander, had two broad choices open to him for the defence of Bangla Desh; to resist the enemy with all his strength and to aim to stop him at the border; or to fight a flexible battle on the border and, if unsuccessful, plan to conduct an organised withdrawal back to ground of his own choosing where he could offer protracted resistance. The former has the advantage, if it succeeds, of not giving up any great extent of territory to the enemy but carries the risk of being defeated in detail at the border. The latter, though it is likely to result in early loss of territory, gives the defender an opportunity of fighting a mobile battle and making the best use of ground.

Although the final decision regarding which course to adopt often depends on political and psychological factors—or the personality of the commander—the most important tactical consideration is the nature of the terrain.

The Terrain

A more detailed topography of Bangla Desh is given in Appendix 'B' to this volume. In general it can be said that Bangla Desh is perhaps the most river-crossed terrain in the world—a land ideal for defensive tactics. Not only do two of the world's great rivers flow through it, tri-secting the country into three geographically isolated sections, a complex criss-cross of minor rivers and rivulets obstruct land movement. Besides, the country in the post-monsoon period can well be described, except perhaps for the north-western salient of Dinajpur-Rangpur, as an almost continuous area of boglands, marshes and watery rice fields.

The width of the two major rivers varies between one and five miles. Destroy the few major bridges (as the Pakistanis did) and an invader has a major problem on his hands.

Every town and village is a defender's dream—and a nightmare for anyone planning offensive operations.

The Defensive Plan

The tactical characteristics stand out clearly. The greatest threat lies from the western and northern sides, not only because of the road approaches from India but also because the grain of the country (the direction of flow of the major rivers) accords with the likely direction of an Indian attack at least upto the line of the Jamuna and the Madhumati rivers. Furthermore, it was here, opposite the western and north-western borders, that the Indian logistical infrastructure—communication networks, ammunition, petrol and supply stocks, medical and other administrative facilities—were the most developed for supporting a major offensive.

From the north, that is the Meghalaya border, the terrain favours movement better than in other parts; however, a major offensive was not likely to develop over the single road-link south from Gauhati to Shillong and the mountain roads thence to the border—particularly as Pakistani Intelligence must have known that there was no great troop build-up on this front.

From the east, the threat from India was also not thought to be a major one because of an almost total lack of infra-structure in the areas around Tripura and Silchar (even as late as in August-September). The railway line from Brahmaputra Valley runs south only as far as Dharamnagar : thence a single road leads south to Agartala and beyond. Clearly no major offensive could develop from this direction either (Niazi could not be expected to have foreseen the tremendous logistical drive set in motion by Eastern Command during September and October to build up stocks of ammunition, petrol and supplies, to improve roads and tracks and to position numerous administrative units. It was only after October that the Pakistanis could have begun to receive indi-cations of troop concentrations in Tripura.)

The plan that Niazi adopted was, as he thought, designed to meet the requirement of imposing maximum delay. It envisaged blocking all routes of entry from India by occupying strong defensive positions along all road approaches and making best use of the terrain, which has been described as one of the most defensible in the world, to hold up the Indian advance. It would mean stretching out his forces along 1,400 miles of border but there were enough troops available to carry out this plan. There were three Pak infantry divisions in Bangla Desh (with a fourth divisional headquarters under raising) and a total of 42 regular battalions each of whom, being American equipped, contained more than twice the light and heavy automatic fire-power of an Indian battalion. The artillery complement was less than normal for Pak Army organisation but still superior to that of the Indian divisions in Eastern Command. There were four or five squadrons of armour (light *Chaffee* tanks) to support the infantry divisions.

With this strong, well-trained force Niazi expected to hold an Indian attack almost indefinitely. He would base his tactical plan on the strong-points along the border, each with concrete pill-boxes, bunkers with six feet thick overhead cover, anti-tank ditches and extensive minefields. A colossal dumping programme had ensured that each point contained enough stocks of ammunition and supplies to hold out for months against the strongest assaults. When our forces eventually captured these strong-points they found pile upon pile of ammunition crates in underground storage chambers, each marked with the famous American aid symbol. At numerous points rivulets were channelled to form moats around the strong-points : and many of these virtual fortresses were held by brigade and battalion groups, each supported by tanks and artillery. (After the operations we were to learn that crores worth of Test Relief funds, meant for refugee relief, had been diverted towards meeting the cost of these constructions. One strong-point alone had used up 29 lakhs of relief funds).

Niazi put his strongest divisions on the western front—opposite Calcutta—and constructed there his most formidable defences, for example the "fortresses" at Jessore and Jenida. 9 Pak Infantry Division, with headquarters at Jessore, was responsible for this sector, south of the Padma and west of Dacca.

In the northern-western sector (north of the Padma and west of the Jamuna) the most strongly defended area was the Dinaj-pur-Rangpur salient, where the going for mobile forces was best. 16 Pak Infantry Division was located in this sector, with Headquarters at Nator, on the Atrai River.

The northern sector was the least strongly held, there being only one brigade deployed forward of Mymensingh. However,

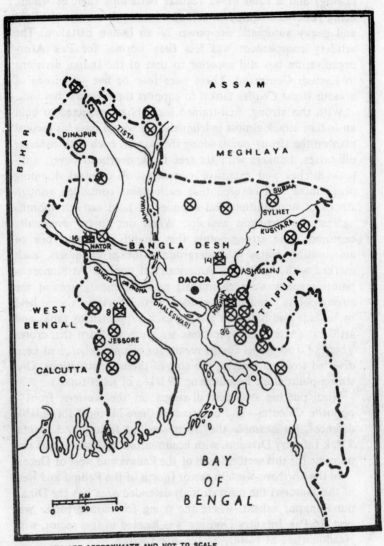

BOUNDARIES ARE APPROXIMATE AND NOT TO SCALE

Pakistani Strongholds in Bangla Desh

in the east, because of the vital Dacca-Comilla-Chittagong road and rail link, a cluster of strongpoints was built at the border with Tripura. Headquarters 14 Pak Infantry Division was located at Ashuganj. The newly raising 36 Pak Division Headquarters was at Comilla—to offset the growing Indian build-up in Tripura.

It will be seen that Niazi pinned all his hopes on stopping the Indian forces on the border. One of the reasons that decided him on this course was that the pattern of Mukti Bahini operations during September and October had convinced him that their primary aim was to liberate a belt of territory inside Bangla Desh all along the border, possibly including some important towns, which would enable them to establish the Bangla Desh government-in-exile on home territory and thus gain diplomatic leverage for seeking recognition. Since Niazi knew that Bangla Desh policy had the support of the Indian government, he assumed that a limited territorial aim was also the policy of India.

It is more than likely that Yahya Khan had ordered Niazi to continue to occupy as much of Bangla Desh as possible, in order to strengthen Pakistan's case at the U.N. Captured Pakistani officers have since confirmed that this political consideration seemed to have been an obsession with the high command—to the detriment of tactical considerations.

Whatever the reason, the fact remains that by the end of November, the Pakistani forces had been committed to a rigid form of linear defence based on "hedge-hog" tactics. Niazi allowed his forces to be drawn out to the border and he depended primarily on the strongpoints holding out. No great military thinker, his plan was negative, rigid and orthodox.

The problem that the Indian General Staff would face, if it came to all-out war, was not only to open the routes into Bangla Desh but to do it with such speed that the enemy would be given no chance of withdrawing and falling back on the great river obstacles, to an inner line of concentrated defence. If the Pak forces could pull back and defend the Dacca "bowl" (the triangle of territory formed by the rivers Jamuna and

Meghna north of Dacca) it would take Eastern Command weeks to crack their defences. Both the rivers are wide at that point and with marshes and boglands all around, Dacca becomes virtually a fortress island. If ever it came to all-out war, it would be imperative that the Indian Army forestall this last-ditch stand by racing for the Dacca "bowl" and beating the enemy to it.

There was a strategic reason also why a war in Bangla Desh had to be concluded within a limited time-frame. Several mountain divisions earmarked for the Chinese front had been re-deployed in Eastern Command for the Bangla Desh task. Some of them would be required back if a Chinese threat developed following a war in Bangla Desh—a possibility that could not be overlooked. The borrowed mountain divisions would be required back quickly.

By training and tradition the Indian Army's normal methods of operation had always been the set-piece battle, phased programmes to capture strong points—and venturing on further advance only after due regrouping and re-inforcement—the classic approach to battle procedure. And that is just what Niazi, brought up in the same tactical tradition, expected the Indian Army to do.

He reckoned without Eastern Army's GOC-in-C, Lieutenant-General J.S. Aurora. For him the task was quite clear, and he was determined to accomplish it; he must get to Dacca within a time-frame of 12–15 days from the declaration of war. Only by adhering to this lightning schedule could he hope to get to his objective before the Pakistani forces pulled back to the inner defence line at the "bowl". It would mean overcoming established tactical concepts and unleashing mobile, flexible thrusts carried out with determination and dash. Our forces would have to throw the enemy into such confusion that before he could resile from the surprise attack, our divisions would begin converging on Dacca. Furthermore, though the Indian forces had overwhelming air superiority, on the ground their superiority ratio was only 7 to 4—much less than the normal 3 to 1 required for an offensive. The strategic plan would have to take this into consideration. It *had* to be a lightning campaign.

General Aurora's tactical concept was as bold as it was simple. The only difficult thing about it would be its execution; for unless it was carried out with drive and determination, accepting calculated risks all along the line, it would flounder amidst pitched battles and phased advances.

The core of the plan was to contain the enemy strongpoints at the border while powerful mobile thrusts, by a series of by-passing moves, cut the enemy's lines of communication and raced ahead for the Dacca "bowl". There would be three major thrusts, one each from each of the three army corps, and a lesser thrust from the Meghalaya area. Each would strive to by-pass major resistance and make for the strategic target, while leaving behind detachments to contain and eventually liquidate centres of resistance. With the cooperation and support of the air and naval arms, he would isolate Dacca from the bulk of the defending army at one full swoop.

Thereafter, General Aurora was going to leave his options open. Not for him the pre-conceived plan of a traditional Phase II. Instead, he would play it off the cuff with the feel of mobile battle in his hands. There would be no pause for re-grouping, no inhibitions about adhering to a rigid plan. Whichever thrust or thrusts looked like being the winner, he would exploit the situation when the time came.

No one was more aware of the difficulties inherent in this unorthodox approach to the battle than "Jaggi" Aurora. No commander before him had ever attempted a war of movement such as this in a land where rivers run to five miles in width, where the going is all infantry—with no scope for fast-moving armoured thrusts, where the enemy was a formidably organised foe with a reputation for fighting as high as that of the army under his command, where the nightmare logistical problems had begun to be solved only a few short weeks before the event.

If it succeeded, it would be only because of the highest standards of command direction and leadership, skill and boldness in execution, and consummate logistical management

BOUNDARIES ARE APPROXIMATE AND NOT TO SCALE

The Lightning Concept

—and the fortitude of his troops. The Army Commander must have had implicit faith in the commanders and troops hurriedly thrown into his command, to have undertaken such a lightning strategic project.

It was difficult for General Aurora to foresee which of his initial thrusts would get to the Dacca "bowl" first. It was a new kind of war he was unleashing; whole brigade groups were to be moved over paddy fields, dragging their impediments behind them; roads were to be avoided; rivers were to be "air-bridged" by helicopter ferry services; rickshaws and cycles were to be used for transporting ammunition and equipment. All these bold concepts carried their own risks— and on their success would depend who would win the race for Dacca.

At the same time, one cannot help feeling that the Eastern Army Commander must have placed his own private bet on the winner : and the denouement, when it came, surprised many on our side as it did the enemy.

Order of Battle

Besides the divisions facing the northern borders in Sikkim and NEFA, General Aurora's Order of Battle consisted of three army corps, a communication zone headquarters that was to act as a mobile, operational formation; and the Mukti Bahini (by then estimated to be about 100,000 strong).

II Corps

Headquarters—Krishnagar
(Lieut-General T.N. Raina)
Two Infantry/Mountain Divisions

Extra allotment of supporting arms* :—

Most of one medium armoured regiment (*T-55s*—Russian)
One Light Tank Regiment (*PT-76* amphibians—Russian)

*Beside artillery and other supporting arms which formed part of the divisions themselves

One Medium Artillery Regiment (130 mm long-range—
Russian)
Engineer (Bridging) units

XXXIII Corps

Headquarters—Siliguri
(Lieut-General M.L. Thapan)
One mountain division
Two extra brigades

Extra allotment of supporting arms :—

One light armoured regiment (*PT-76s*—Russian)
One medium artillery regiment (British 5.5 inch)
Engineer (Bridging) units

101 Communication Zone
Headquarters—Gauhati
(Major-General G.S. Gill)*
One infantry brigade.

IV Corps

Headquarters—Agartala
(Lieut-General Sagat Singh)
Three mountain divisions

Extra allotment of supporting arms :—

Two *ad hoc* squadrons of light armour (*PT-76s*—Russian)
One medium artillery regiment (British 5.5 inch)

Apart from the above, the ground forces were allotted a
given number of air sorties for close support which would
increase considerably—almost to an "as required" scale—
when the PAF in Bangla Desh had been neutralised.

*After General Gill was wounded, Major G.S. Nagra took command.

The total strength of the forces assembled for the Bangla Desh liberation, including the Mukti Bahini and the administrative units spread over West Bengal, Assam and Tripura, exceeded a third of a million. The northern divisions facing Tibet accounted for another 100,000 or so—the overall figure in Eastern Command nearing half a million men.

No Lieutenant-General in military history has commanded so large an army or borne so heavy a strategic responsibility.

CHAPTER VII

Twelve Days to Dacca

Mrs Indira Gandhi was in Calcutta on the evening of 3 December when she received news of the Pakistani attack in the west. Not long afterwards her aircraft took off from Dum Dum airport, heading for Delhi. Later the same night, General Aurora received the "go-ahead" from Army Head-quarters.

Eastern Command Headquarters had been toned up to a pitch of efficiency that would enable it dexterously to handle the war of movement the GOC-in-C was unleashing. It would not be feasible to control this fast-moving operation by the issue of customary, formal written orders; even signal messages, which had to be coded and decoded, would at times be too cumbersome. If the commanders in the field were to be kept on the go, to maintain the momentum of the offensive, they would have to receive their instructions by telephone or wire-less, on the spur of the moment. The teamwork in Head-quarters, and in the whole Command, was such that in the event this informality of approach worked to a nicety.

By daybreak on 4 October, the liberation campaign was under way.

On the II Corps front opposite the Calcutta region, General Raina sent in two divisional thrusts towards the Madhumati river, which takes off from the Padma at Kushtia and flows almost due south into the Sunderban delta west of Barisal. The aim on this front was to liberate territory west of the Padma. II Corps planned to achieve this by containing Pak strongholds near the border while fast-moving columns

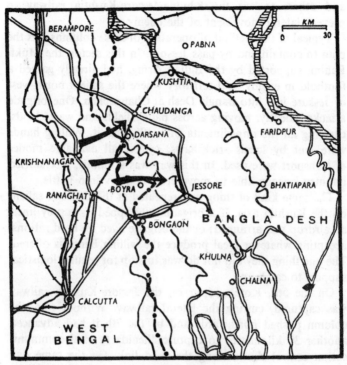

II Corps Thrusts

by-passed them and raced for the Madhumati, to prevent the bulk of the enemy from withdrawing across the river and making for the Meghna ferries to Dacca.

The Corps plan was to spread the two divisional thrusts into several columns, one making for Kushtia, one for Magura and Faridpur on the Jessore axis, one for Khulna and Barisal and others to cut the Khulna-Jessore-Kushtia railway to prevent lateral movement of the enemy.

Typical of the method of operation of these columns was the plan to contain and by-pass Jessore. In this sector, the Mukti Bahini, supported by the Indian Army, had already gained a foothold in enemy held territory where the salient north-west of Jessore juts into Bangla Desh at Chaugachha. One brigade attacked silently, moving across paddy fields and waste lands, carrying all the impedimenta of battle with it. Willing hands were lent by locals—rickshaws, cycles, all available modes of transport were used. In this way was a mobile, mechanised infantry brigade able to move cross-country into battle.

The same kind of thing was repeated at the Darsana salient on the Kushtia axis. If a brigade outstripped its supply lines, an airdrop was arranged; or the brigade lived on hard rations, accepting whatever local produce the willing Bengalis offered. The one thing they did not do was to stop for regular logistical support to catch up.

On the 5th, Kotchandpur on the Jessore-Kushtia railway was captured, cutting the lateral railway. Without rest, the column pushed northwards and by the 7th it had advanced another 30 kilometres to capture Jhenida (a vital communication centre) thus cutting the road link. On the same day Jessore was vacated by the enemy—who pulled out helter-skelter for Magura (on the Madhumati). The subsequent capture of Meherpur opened the way to Chuadanga and Kushtia.

The evacuation of Jessore provided one instance of the degeneration of the Pakistani army. This stronghold was defended by an infantry brigade group supported by tanks and artillery—some 5,000 men. It was one of the most strongly fortified positions in Bangla Desh, the Headquarters of Pakistan's 9 Infantry Division. Yet when the time came to fight, the whole garrison turned tail and ran. In the words of Philip Jacobson of the *Sunday Times* :

The total collapse of the Pakistani army's resistance in Jessore is one

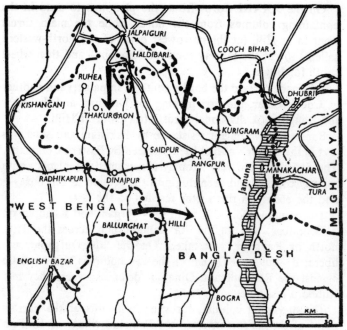

BOUNDARIES ARE APPROXIMATE AND NOT TO SCALE

XXXIII Corps Thrusts

of the most intriguing puzzles of the war in the east. For weeks Indian Army sources and other expert observers had been predicting that ,a stern siege, involving heavy Indian casualties, would be needed to take the Jessore Cantonment—a vast military complex covering an area of several miles just outside Jessore town....

Instead, in the stinging words of Colonel P.S. Deshpande...of the 9th Indian Division: "They ran away." In less than 24 hours, Indian tanks and infantry took an objective they had estimated might require upto a week's bitter fighting.

On the **XXXIII** Corps front, the plan was to send in the containing columns from the north while the main thrust went in at Hilli (at the narrowest point of the north-western salient) to cut the railway south of Rangpur—and then wheel south for Bogra.

A brigade crossed the border south of Jalpaiguri and another at Cooch Bihar, the first making for Dinajpur and the other for Rangpur. A divisional thrust struck out at Hilli.

Some of the strongest resistance by Pakistani garrisons was met in this sector—as had been foreseen by Eastern Command. The defences were very strongly constructed; in places entire railway coaches had been dug into the ground as pill boxes— and the enemy in this sector resisted to the last.

The columns from the north took Pirganj and Khanpur on 5 December; and on the 7th Lalmunirhat, across the Tista north of Rangpur, was taken. On the 8th, Durgapur was liberated—but by 9 December the two columns had come up against the Rangpur and Dinajpur defences, where they met stubborn resistance.

The divisional column, thrusting eastwards at the narrow point of the salient, invested the Pakistan village of Hilli on the 6th—the commencement of a bitter struggle. The Pakistan garrison virtually had to be annihilated before the post could be taken. A part of the Indian column by-passed Hilli and made for Palashbari, 35 kilometres east of Hilli, which it captured on the 9th.

In the 101 Communication Zone area, the main strike was from Tura towards Jamalpur, some 50 kilometres up the river, northwest, from Mymensingh. The enemy in this sector had deployed one infantry brigade, supported by a squadron of tanks—the brigade headquarters and two battalions in Mymensingh, one battalion in Jamalpur. The enemy must have had intelligence of the Indian deployment plan and must have known that there was only one brigade on the whole Meghalaya front at Tura.

By 9 December, the brigade from Tura was on the outskirts of Jamalpur. A by-passing column crossed the Brahmaputra

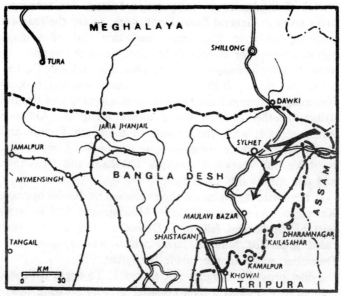

BOUNDARIES ARE APPROXIMATE AND NOT TO SCALE

IV Corps Offensive in Sylhet District

and cut off Jamalpur on 9 December. The enemy then re-inforced the Jamalpur garrison with one battalion from the brigade in Mymensingh.

In the IV Corps sector, in the east, the plan was to send in three divisional thrusts across the 250-kilometre stretch of border between Meghalaya in the north and the Feni salient in the extreme south of Tripura.

IV Corps task was to liberate all Bangla Desh territory south of the Surma and east of the Meghna rivers. The strongest army corps in General Aurora's army, it had the longest stretch of the border as its operational front. The subsidiary tasks given to General Sagat Singh were: to cut the road-rail communication to Chittagong and thus seal off a major supply channel for Bangla Desh; and, when the opportunity arose, to force a crossing of the Meghna and make for Dacca.

General Sagat Singh planned to carry out his task by launching a division from the Silchar-Karimganj area towards Sylhet; another division would attack along the Akhaura-Ashuganj axis; while the division in the south Tripura area would send in three columns—one to contain Comilla, one to strike out westwards towards Laksham and Chandpur, and one southwards from Feni.

In the north, the divisional thrust crossed the border opposite Karimganj and struck eastwards. Munshinagar, 15 kilometres west of the border, fell on 5 December. One column then raced south for Maulavi Bazar which was captured on 8 December, while another made for Sylhet.

Sylhet proved a tougher nut to crack. To begin with, the column had to effect a river crossing with no bridging equipment immediately available. A demand for helicopters brought immediate response and one of the first "air bridging" operations of the war was carried out during the hours of darkness.

By next morning, the column was knocking at the gates of Sylhet.

In his central sector, IV Corps Commander launched a division from the Agartala area towards Akhaura. At this point of the border, the Mukti Bahini had already obtained a lodgment inside Bangla Desh and was in contact with the Pak defences at Akhaura.

It is apparent that this was the division with which General Sagat Singh planned to "bounce" across the Meghna and race for the Dacca "bowl". The Meghna would prove a considerable obstacle—more than a mile wide in the stretch between Shaistaganj and Bhairab Bazar. The railway line from Akhaura went north-westwards towards the Ashuganj rail bridge over Meghna. There was no proper road following the line of the railway and it was only to be expected that the

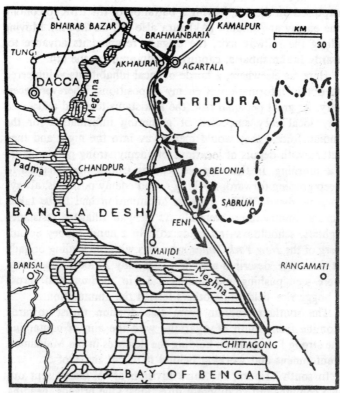

BOUNDARIES ARE APPROXIMATE AND NOT TO SCALE

The Main IV Corps Thrust from Tripura

enemy would blow the rail bridge before the Indian forces could get to it. Despite these difficulties, the Corps Commander was determined to beat the time-table and get to Dacca first.

The leading brigade encircled Akhaura and moved on towards the nearby township of Ganganagar, which they captured on the 5th, leaving a battalion of the EBR to contain the enemy at Akhaura (Akhaura also fell on the 5th). Moving along the railway axis, the brigade resumed its advance towards Brahmanbaria, capturing Sultanpur on the 6th.

Here, as elsewhere, a horde of local inhabitants volunteered to obtain information of enemy dispositions, wherever necessary. At great personal risk (the Pakistanis tortured and killed any local they suspected of gathering information for the Indian forces) they would melt away into the night and then return with details of locations of enemy strong-points before the morning. In this way our leading troops were enabled to keep groping forward, working round enemy positions, always forging ahead. Where guns or ammunition had to be taken across country, there were always Bengali villagers, resistance fighters, schoolboys—all ready to help a hand. Sidney Schanberg of the *New York Times,* who was with the leading brigade at this stage, describes a scene where fully 20 local inhabitants were seen pushing and pulling a 5.5 in. medium gun across a boggy rice field while others ferried the ammunition.

The southern column from this division thrust towards Comilla from south of Agartala, with the aim of containing the strong Pak garrison holding the defences in the Mainamati Cantonment and working behind it to cut the l of c.

In south Tripura, the third division of IV Corps sent out two columns in two different directions. One brigade, heading westwards, made for the important rail junction at Laksham, another headed south for Chittagong.

By the 8th, the fifth day of the war, Brahmanbaria had fallen, Comilla was encircled and the Laksham column was heading for Chandpur. The whole of the sector opposite Tripura came under Indian control, while in the south—where the Feni salient had already been liberated before the commencement of the war—a column from the southern division raced south for Chittagong.

Air and Naval Operations

While the Army was making spectacular progress in Bangla

Desh territory, the support provided by the IAF and the Indian Navy (IN) reached a level never experienced before in India.

The main tasks of Eastern Air Command were: the air defence of West Bengal; bomber operations (in the interdiction role—that is, destruction of enemy 1 of c to isolate their forward troops); close support of the ground forces; and air transport operations. The first two could be termed strategic tasks, the third tactical and the fourth logistical support. However, whatever the strategic priority, Eastern Air Command had ensured that a certain number of sorties would at all times be available to the divisional commanders on the ground for the close support of forward troops.

The enemy was known to have a squadron of about 18 *Sabre Jets* in Bangla Desh: at one time a number of *MIG-19s* had been reported seen on the Dacca airbase but either they had pulled back to the west or the report had been false. In any event, no *MIG-19* was ever encountered in this theatre.

Eastern Air Command neutralised the PAF in Bangla Desh by the end of the second day of the war. Although some *Sabres* survived the air battles and the bombing, the PAF was never again in evidence over the scene of battle. This was one of the greatest factors in enabling the Indian columns to race ahead; thereafter there were no restrictions on movement, dispersion, camouflage, density of vehicles on the road or digging in of gun positions. Columns could push ahead as best as they could, without danger of air strafing—something that armies dream about.

The number of sorties available for close support also increased considerably. In fact there were times when sorties were going a-begging; the forward troops were racing ahead so fast that they could seldom wait for an air strike to be arranged. It was only when a strong-point had to be taken that air strikes were in demand—but even in those cases the number of ground support sorties after 5 December averaged 120 per day. A remarkable feature of the air strikes was that the bombing of fortifications was carried out with such absolute precision that virtually no damage was caused to civilians or non-military structures—at Jessore, Kushtia, Khulna and many other centres of resistance.

At Jhenida, where an infantry brigade had outstripped its maintenance column, the IAF hurriedly arranged an air drop of supplies and ammunition. Wherever necessary, casualties were evacuated by the Air Force—by helicopter and light aircraft. But the most spectacular use of the transport wing of the IAF came with the necessity for river-crossing operations. A whole fleet of *MI-4* helicopters worked round the clock to "air bridge" the rivers of Bangla Desh—at Sylhet, in Magura on the Madhumati, across the Meghna in the famous Ashuganj crossing and on a number of other occasions. Men, guns, ammunition—all were ferried across helter-skelter, to enable the leading columns to race towards their goal.

A special task in the interdiction programme was the strafing of rivercraft along the numerous waterways. As the Indian columns thrust past the strongholds and struck deeper into Bangla Desh, more and more Pakistani personnel, particularly from rear areas, were abandoning their posts and slipping away in whatever form of transport they could find on the waterways; luxurious river steamers (that were once the pride of the old East Bengal Railway steamer service to Dacca) patrol boats, large country craft, small boats, commercial carrier flats and even rafts. The IAF kept up a ceaseless series of strikes against these escaping groups, sinking some 270 craft of various types before the end of the war.

In this war in the air, both strategic and tactical support missions were shared with the Navy's Fleet Air Arm operating from the aircraft carrier *Vikrant*. The line dividing the operations of the two Services was the latitude 21° N. The Navy's responsibility lay south of that latitude.

One of the first targets of the Fleet Air Arm was Chittagong, where both the airport and the seaport were attacked. Other aerial targets attacked by the *Vikrant's* aircraft were Chalna, Mungla, Barisal and Cox's Bazar in the extreme south-east.

The main task of the Eastern Naval Command was, of course, the sealing of Bangla Desh ports to prevent any naval craft either from entering or leaving those waters—and in this it succeeded beyond all expectation.

The International Front

On December 6, Mrs Gandhi announced in the Indian Parliament that Government of India had accorded recognition to the Bangla Desh government.

The attitude of President Nixon—always strongly pro-Pak military junta—had hardened against India even before the outbreak of war, when Pakistani forces were being put more and more on the defensive by Mukti Bahini activities and the Indian Army's overt support of its operations. He ordered cancellation of all remaining export licences for military equipment to India (some six crores worth).

After Pakistan's attack in the west, a State Department spokesman placed "the major responsibility for broader operations" on India—and hastened to take the issue to the Security Council. The State Department was consistently bullied by the White House into "tilting" its approach in favour of Pakistan. However, the Russian veto foiled all President Nixon's efforts to help his ally.

The disclosures made by Mr Jack Anderson of the secret proceedings of National Security Council (NSC) WASAG meetings* under Dr Kissinger's chairmanship clearly reveal the extent of the White House conspiracy to misrepresent facts regarding the aggression by Pakistan. As Mr Tom Wicker of the *New York Times* has commented: "The (Anderson) papers make one thing quite clear—that President Nixon, with the aid of Dr Kissinger, set out deliberately to put the United States in a position of support for Pakistan at whatever cost."

A harsh State Department statement, issued with the concurrence of President Nixon, blamed India for the war in Bangla Desh: "We believe that since the beginning of the crisis, Indian policy in a systematic way has led to perpetuation

*Washington Special Action Group of the NSC.

of the crisis, a deepening of the crisis, and that India
bears the major responsibility for the broader hostilities
which have ensued." There was no mention of the savage
policies pursued by the Pakistan military regime nor of its
open aggression on the western front (though special concern was always expressed at the WASAG meetings for Pakistanis and Biharis in Bangla Desh).

There was, fortunately for India, greater understanding
of the Bangla Desh tragedy elsewhere in the United States.
On 7 December, Senator Edward Kennedy made a speech in
the Senate assailing the Administration's stand: "The war
did not begin last week with military border crossings, or last
month with the escalation of artillery crossfire. This was
begun on the bloody night of 25 March with the brutal suppression by the Pakistani army of the results of a free election."
Senator Muskie, the leading candidate for the Democratic
Party's Presidential nomination, took very much the same
line—as did other Democrats.

On the same day, the General Assembly of the UN passed
a resolution by 104 votes to 11 calling for a ceasefire and immediate withdrawal of troops by both sides. The overwhelming
vote against her was a new experience for India—but it reflected the pressure brought by America on the smaller states
of Afro-Asia: it was the voting of the big powers that counted.
Russia voted against the resolution; Britain and France
abstained; America and China supported it.

Diplomatic pressure was not the only action President
Nixon was planning to take. Orders were already going out
across the Pacific to mobilise the mighty Seventh Fleet, "the
most powerful force in the world", to mobilise for action in
the Bay of Bengal. If UN resolutions would not deter the
Indians from the liberation campaign, they would have to be
intimidated and, if necessary, deterred by the armed might
of the most powerful nation in the world.

The task force from the 7th US Fleet was of formidable
strength. The flagship was the 90,000 ton nuclear-powered
"Attack" aircraft-carrier *Enterprise,* capable of launching

Phantom fighter-bombers carrying nuclear war-heads. The second aircraft-carrier was a "Commando helicopter launcher", the *Tripoli*. There were six other warships, including destroyers, destroyer escorts and administrative elements.

While it was put about by White House apologists that this super flotilla was being sent out to evacuate a handful of Americans, mostly missionaries (who had refused to be flown out when other American nationals were evacuated) in fact the operational task given to the 7th Fleet was, as summarised by Mr Anderson from NSC records:

> To compel India to divert both ships and planes to shadow the task force;
>
> To weaken India's blockade against East Pakistan;
>
> Possibly to divert the Indian aircraft-carrier *Vikrant* from its military mission;
>
> To force India to keep planes on defence alert, thus reducing their operations against Pakistani ground troops.

The Ring Closes In

While IV Corps' columns in the east were racing for Dacca and Chittagong, General Raina's II Corps struck out for the line of the Madhumati. The northern division sent two columns towards Magura, the only likely crossing place on the Madhumati, while the southern division wheeled south after capturing Jessore and made for Khulna.

An eye-witness account of the southern column's progress describes a typical day's fighting in this sector:

> The gruesome trail that marked the headlong retreat of the Pakistani Army from its "impregnable" position in Jessore began a few miles outside the town. The tarmac road was scarred and furrowed by machine-gun bullets and rockets. A dozen burnt-out jeeps and lorries lay twisted in the ditches at their side. Then, the bodies: Pakistani regulars frozen in grotesque poses of agony. Some were charred and blackened, others had terrible, fly-covered wounds.
>
> They were the first dead Pakistani soldiers we had seen in this sector since the war began. They had been caught by Indian tanks tearing

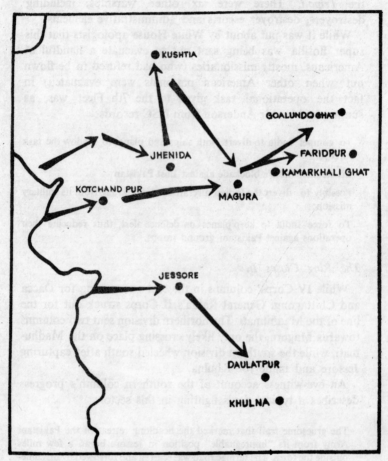

Progress on the Jessore front—11 December

through Jessore and by jet fighters: they had abandoned their vehicles and run vainly for the ditches. A large and cheerful crowd of locals posed proudly around the corpses, right arms erect in the "Joi Bangla!" salute.

A mile further down the road were the remains of Rupadia, a hamlet unlucky enough to be the scene of a delaying action by Pakistani infantry, desperately covering the rear of a 2,000-strong column which included almost 1,000 wives and families of officers, formerly stationed at Jessore. The flattened huts were still burning and three buses used for a barricade had been raked with bullets from end to end.

Moving forward through a battalion of the Madrasi Regiment—small, cheerful men who waved and smiled at everyone—our photographer Penny Tweedie and I hitched a short ride on a Russian-built *T-55* tank of the Indian 63rd Cavalry. Clanking and grinding up the narrow road, ducking the big 105 mm gun as it swivelled to point towards Pakistani positions, we arrived at the foremost point of the Indian advance. A full squadron of 15 *T-55s* was assembling to support the Madrasis in their next push down the Khulna road. Crouching nervously behind the comforting bulk of the tanks every time a shell from the Pakistanis 105 mm guns landed anywhere remotely near us, we watched Indian advance units carefully probing the enemy's positions. A company of Pakistani infantrymen—probably from the 27th Baluch Regiment—was holding up the advance with mortar and machinegun fire; the sound of small arms fire could be heard clearly a few hundred yards away.

When shelling failed to dislodge the Pakistani rearguard, the local commander Lt. Col. Naregyen—an amiable, imperturbable Madrasi—decided to call for air support. Radios crackled impressively and map references were busily exchanged and checked.

Everyone looked expectantly upwards. Nothing happened for a while. Then, quite suddenly, two of the Indian Air Force's Russian *SU-7* fighters appeared high in the enormous blue sky. For a few minutes they circled gracefully, like hawks searching for prey.

Then, after a tank fired a blue smoke-maker shell, they banked into a steep dive and straightened out at tree-top level. From where we stood, I could see the flashes from the big .30 calibre machine guns as the jets strafed Pakistani positions.

When the planes turned away for their base near Calcutta, the Pakistani guns had been silenced. The tanks roared into life again and crashed away through the bright-yellow mustard fields, followed by the Madrasi infantry. "Khulna is finished", Colonel Naregyen shouted as he sped away in his command jeep.*

The Sunday Times (London).

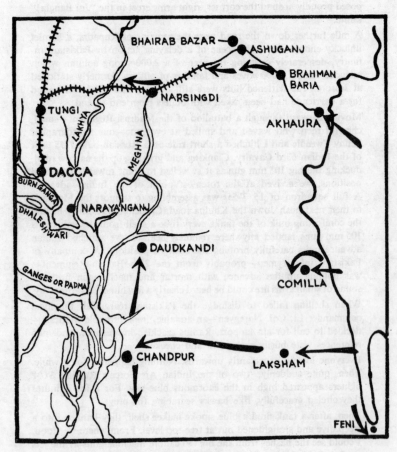

Progress on the IV Corps front—12 December

By December, the two columns from the northern division of II Corps had by-passed the Pakistani garrison at Magura and reached the outskirts of Kamarkhali Ghat on the Madhumati. Kamarkhali is a vital crossing point on the river because across it lies the town of Mahukhali which controls the routes to both Faridpur and Goalundo Ghat on the Padma (or Ganga). Here a delay was caused by lack of river-crossing equipment. Advance parties and patrols made use of local country-boats, which the villagers willingly produced, but the main column had to wait for the fleet of helicopters sent in by the IAF to "air-bridge" the Indian force across the river.

By the 14th, leading elements of the Indian columns had reached Faridpur on the Padma. On the Khulna axis, Daulatpur (a few miles north of Khulna) was taken. The main escape route of the Pakistani troops in the Kushtia-Jessore-Khulna sector had been sealed off.

In the north-western sector, progress made by the northern thrusts was still slow because of strong resistance by the defenders. Lalmunirhat, north-west of Rangpur, had fallen a few days previously—giving the Indian forces control of the Tista crossings. It was the main offensive at Hilli, however, that forged ahead. By the 12th Ghoraghat had been captured and from there the column wheeled south, aiming for Bogra. A strong group of Mukti Bahini was operating in this region and with their help Gobindpur half-way between Ghoraghat and Bogra, was liberated. On 14th December, Bogra, the divisional headquarters of the Pakistani forces was captured and the Indian column moved southwards for Sherpur and beyond.

On IV Corps front in the east the main threat to Dacca was being posed. On 9 December, the thrust from Akhaura had reached the Meghna at Ashuganj, where the rail bridge crosses over the Meghna. Two spans of the bridge had been destroyed: the Meghna was now a formidable obstacle, nearly a mile wide.

The leading brigade began reconnoitering for a crossing place. Hundreds of villagers had volunteered to help, bringing

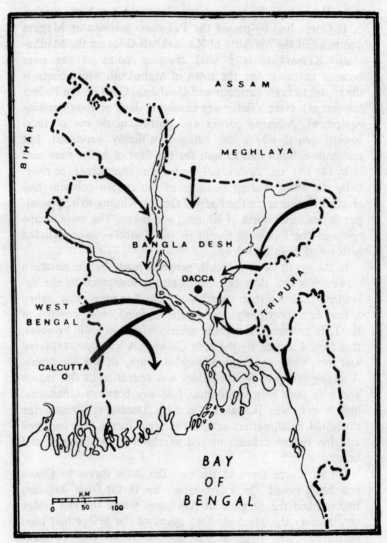

Isolating the Dacca "Bowl"

boats and rafts. Assault elements soon crossed over, but to enable the brigade to conduct operations across the river the supporting artillery and its ammunition, recoilless anti-tank guns and other pieces of heavy equipment would have to be taken across. There was also the problem of the PT-76 tanks. Although they were amphibian, Russian designers had not catered for the rivers of Bangla Desh: the tanks were known to overheat after half-an-hour of "swimming", and the crossing of the wide, swift-flowing Meghna could take anything up to three hours. In the end the tanks were launched into the river, moved under their own power as long as possible and then towed and pushed across by hordes of country boats.

The helicopter "air-bridging" operation started on the 10th. The 'bridge builders' worked incessantly, ferrying whatever equipment could not be taken across in country boats. By the 11th, there was a sufficient force on the far side to resume the advance. The crossing had taken place about two miles south of the bridge site. The strong enemy garrison at Bhairab Bazar made no move to oppose the crossing, though they could not have helped observing the helicopters in action. Fear of the Mukti Bahini as well as their own demoralised state kept them in their bunkers.

There was no road axis leading out from the bridge-head towards Dacca—and the Indian column had to strike out across country along the railway line, by-passing Bhairab Bazar. Again local civilians turned out by the hundreds to lend a hand with the heavy equipment. On reaching the railway tracks, an enterprising artillery captain, who knew something about diesel engines, found an abandoned goods train on the line and promptly set about loading his guns on the flats. Before long he had the train moving and soon caught up with the brigade column.

On the same day, the southern column had broken through Laksham and captured Chandpur, a port on the main Padma river south of Dacca and Narayanganj. A column was imme-diately sent north from Chandpur towards Daukhandi on the Meghna.

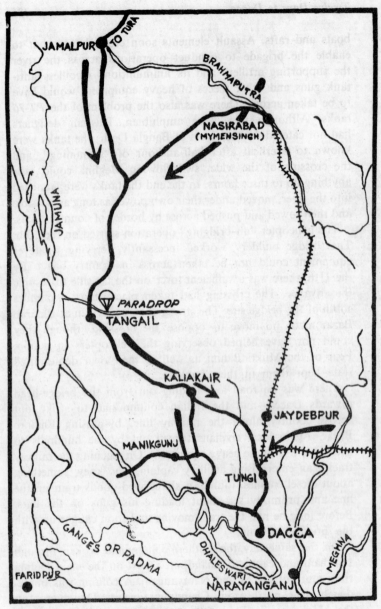

Trump Card at Tangail

The Trump Card

The Army Commander, watching the progress of the campaign from his Operations Room in Fort William, had every cause to be satisfied. By the 11th, it had become obvious that his plan had succeeded: the greater part of the Pakistani forces in the three regions, west and south of Padma and west of the Meghna, had been encircled and their retreat to the Dacca "bowl" cut off. Only in the Mymensingh sector between the Padma was there any possibility of the Pak Army withdrawing more or less intact.

While there was only one enemy brigade in this sector this brigade, together with the Pak forces withdrawing from the Ashuganj front, would be a considerable re-inforcement for the Dacca garrison—where there was reckoned to be a total of some 5,000 assorted troops but no regular infantry formation. It was not that Dacca was expected to hold out for long: there could be little doubt in General Aurora's mind about its eventual capture. What he feared was the widespread destruction and loss of civilian lives that would result if the battle for the city lasted for even a few days—not to mention the savage reprisals that the Pakistani troops would inflict on the inhabitants, as indeed they had already carried out in a number of places. Somehow he must prevent the northern Pak garrison from reaching Dacca.

On the afternoon of 11th December, a number of UN aircraft had touched down at Dum Dum airport, carrying foreign evacuees from Dacca. Present at the scene were foreign and Indian journalists. They saw a whole fleet of IAF transports lined up on the tarmac—Russian *AN-12s*, Canadian *Caribous,* American *Farichild Packets* and *Dakotas*—and a mass of paratroopers emplaning. The word went round that a whole parachute brigade was about to take off on a mission—and no one contradicted the rumour. By the next morning word would reach Dacca—re-inforced by reports of other paratroopers emplaning in Air India's *Boeing 737s* from Barrackpore. (These latter were the first lot of forces to move westwards from Eastern Command, but it did no harm to let Niazi assume that thousands of Indian paratroopers were about to descend on Dacca.)

On the Mymensingh front, the Indian brigade investing Jamalpur had sent one battalion across the Jamuna and cut the road behind the defenders. General Nagra had also brought up another brigade which was making for Mymensingh. There was, however, no certainty as yet that the Pak brigade would not be able to extricate itself and withdraw to Dacca via Tangail. The Army Commander decided not to take any chances.

At Tangail, a small enemy garrison was holding the defences, acting as "caretakers" for the brigade in Mymensingh which was expected to fall back and fight on from the Tangail defences. It will be remembered that the Tangail area was also the head-quarters of "Tiger" Siddiqi's powerful group of Mukti Bahini guerillas, which had virtual control of all the countryside. It was decided to capture Tangail by a paradrop which would make contact with the guerillas, cut off the enemy retreat and hold on until a link-up could take place with the Indian brigades in the north.

A battalion of an Indian Parachute Brigade, together with its supporting arms (mountain and recoilless anti-tank guns) was para-dropped in the Tangail area on the afternoon of 11 December—just in time. As the battalion commander was later to learn from Brigadier Qadir, the Pak Brigade Commander at Mymensingh General Niazi had already ordered the brigade to withdraw to Dacca: in fact, the first vehicle column had passed through Tangail heading south earlier that afternoon.

After a dummy drop to the southwest of the town, the actual drop took place in the open plain across a river which flows east to west a few miles north of Tangail. The main tasks of the Para Battalion were to capture the bridge and the ferry site across the river to prevent any enemy escaping towards the south; to capture Tangail; to link up with the local detachments of "Tiger" Siddiqi's Mukti Bahini guerillas; and, finally, after linking up with the Indian brigade moving south from Jamalpur, to move towards Dacca under orders of GOC 101 Communication Zone.

Dropping from a height of 1,000–1,200 feet in a keen 12-knot breeze, the battalion's spread on the ground was somewhat larger than the 2 kilometres by 1 kilometre dropping zone it had planned. That was not the only *contretemps*. The countryside, while generally flat, is dotted with clusters of villages, each with its own pond, as is normally found in Bengal. The Commanding Officer of the battalion came splashing down in the middle of one and had to swim his way out. A few mountain and recoilless guns also landed in ponds. Other parachutes, carrying both men and equipment, landed on tops of village huts.

The battalion, in true Para Brigade tradition, took all this in its stride. Within two hours, the men and equipment had been reformed into their platoons and companies, and were moving off to carry out their various tasks. It was pitch dark by then but there was a host of willing helpers among the villagers who volunteered not only to guide the troops to their objectives but also to bring food and water for the officers and men.

While the main body of the battalion moved towards the bridge, one company was sent to hold the ferry site; a partol was sent northwards up the Jamalpur road to give warning of enemy approach.

The first sign of the enemy was a small vehicle column coming from the direction of Jamalpur which made contact with the patrol two miles north of the bridge. After a brief exchange of fire, the column withdrew.

The next column, a larger one, came down the Mymensingh road with full headlights on (the Mymensingh road joins the Jamalpur road a few miles north of the bridge). This column was allowed to come right up to the battalion position and the first three vehicles were knocked out by rocket launchers. About 30 Pak troops were killed in the process. This was the Pak Light Battery of artillery withdrawing from Mymensingh. The remainder of the column, strung out on the road behind, turned around and sped back.

When the Pakistanis realised that Indian forces had captured Tangail, they mounted several attacks to open the route to Dacca. Three night attacks on the bridge and on the dropping zone (where collection of equipment was still continuing) were repulsed. There was one last desperate assault mounted by the Pak troops in broad daylight the following morning—resulting only in slaughter. The Pakistani soldiers were virtually leaderless by then, their officers having abandoned them during the night and slipped away across country towards Dacca. The attacks ceased thereafter and many of the enemy troops gave themselves up, while others melted away into the surrounding country. Later the battalion was to count 223 bodies left behind by the fleeing Pakistanis.

That was the end of the road for Qadir's brigade. Very few got back to Dacca: Qadir himself surrendered later in the day.

The scene in Tangail, as in every other liberated town or village in Bangla Desh, was one of joyful tears, the inhabitants hardly able to contain their overwhelming emotion. For a while it was difficult for the battalion to set about its task, so tumultuous was the ovation and reception accorded to the Indians.

When an officer wanted to thank a Bengali lady who had fed the men of his company at her house she said: "There is no need for thanks. Please just do me one favour—never ask me or people like me what the Pakistanis have done to us."

Later in the day, the Indian brigade coming down the Jamalpur road linked up with the paratroopers; soon after it came General Nagra, the GOC, and his tactical headquarters.

The GOC's plans were to push ahead as fast as possible for Dacca. He sent the leading brigade down the road, to Joydebpur; a second brigade was due to follow up in a few hours. The Para Battalion was ordered to remain temporarily in Tangail.

On the 13th the leading troops were held up at Joydebpur, where there was some resistance. The second brigade then passed through and took over the advance. They forced a crossing over a river which delayed them a few hours, but were soon pushing south towards Tungi.

On the 14th, the GOC decided on a new tack. Just east of Kaliakair a newly built highway unmarked on the map takes off southwards. Informed by the locals that this road linked up with the "Khulna—Dacca Highway" and led into Dacca, via Manikgang, from the west, General Nagra decided to place his bet on this axis and pushed the now completely re-grouped Para Battalion down this road.

Thus it was that in the early morning of 16 December, as dawn was breaking, the leading elements of the Para Battalion came on the outskirts of Dacca, exactly 12 days after the first Indian troops crossed the Bangla Desh border on their historic mission of liberation.

CHAPTER VIII

Surrender at Dacca

By 11 December, Pakistani troops had begun to surrender in certain sectors. The writing was on the wall—and those who chose to read it took the wisest course. There would be much fanatical resistance in some places, even desperate suicidal assaults; but the inevitability of defeat had struck home by then.

In Dacca, Major-General Farman Ali flashed an appeal to the United Nations pleading with the Security Council to arrange for the evacuation of Pakistani troops and official civilians to Pakistan—in return for which he offered the establishment of elected government in Bangla Desh. This was an extraordinary step to take. Farman Ali's official designation was Military Adviser to the Governor, who apparently had been by-passed. In any case, Farman Ali was junior in rank to Niazi—and later Niazi made it clear that he had not authorised any such approach to the UN by Farman Ali.

The probable explanation is that Farman Ali, an impressive looking but somewhat sinister figure, was probably the power behind the occupation government in Dacca. If so, he would have been responsible for enforcing the campaign of savagery against the people of Bangla Desh. It would be natural for him to want to escape at the first signs of possible defeat. Whatever the case, his last minute bid to escape failed; barely had the Security Council begun to consider Farman Ali's appeal when it received a message from Yahya Khan countermanding the request.

Taking advantage of the split in Pakistani High Command,

the Indian Army Chief, General Manekshaw, broadcast his first message to the enemy commander in Dacca, advising surrender. This was the first of three messages sent by General Manekshaw, each stressing the humanitarian aspect and guaranteeing observance of the Geneva Convention regarding treatment of prisoners of war. As General Niazi later stated, it was this factor that most affected his final decision.

At the same time, India stepped up her psychological campaign to break down Pakistani morale in Dacca—if indeed there was any morale left beyond bluster. Reports emanating from the Intercontinental Hotel, which had been declared a neutral zone to shelter foreign residents, told of the craven behaviour of senior officers and officials—frantic to seek asylum or somehow to get out of Dacca. It was also reported that a number of civil aircrafts had already taken off, carrying Special Intelligence Service personnel (the worst among the exterminators) and other officials to Akyab. Now, it became imperative to prevent the Dacca garrison from holding out a day longer than necessary; the reprisals enforced by that dehumanised, defeated soldiery would be no less brutal in the face of certain defeat.

Military targets in Dacca were constantly pounded by the IAF and a stream of confusing messages were sent over the Pak Army wireless channels—all designed to bewilder the enemy. The Indian "electronic warfare" programme had broken the Pakistani code, so that enemy communications were easily intercepted—and appropriate action was taken further to erode morale.

By land, the pressure was no less determined. The western and north-western sectors had been liberated and the retreating Pak forces encircled. In the north-east, the entire garrison at Sylhet, under command of Brigadier Rana of the Pak Army, had surrendered and the Indian forces were moving swiftly southwards.

The leading troops of IV Corps had reached Narsingdi, on the Ashuganj-Tungi railway, on the evening of the 14th and were pressing forward to Tungi.

It was, however, the Para Battalion from Tangail, who beat everyone to Dacca. Redirected by the GOC on to the Kliakair-Manikganj road, the battalion raced ahead and by dawn on 16 December, the head of the column was leaning against Dacca—having come to within two miles of the city. Here the GOC, General Gandharv Nagra, joined the Paratroopers.

Gandharv Nagra had been, some years before, Military Adviser to the Indian High Commission in Karachi—when Niazi was a brigade commander in Sind. He had known Niazi and now he decided to contribute his mite toward softening up the Pak General. He sent his ADC, accompanied by the adjutant of the Para Battalion, in a jeep under a truce flag, with a message for Niazi—a message that was to echo around the newsworld:

> My dear Abdullah, I am here. The game is up. I suggest you give yourself up to me and I'll look after you.

It was common knowledge that surrender in the east was imminent—a simple case of deductive reasoning; but the actual timing, the channels through which Niazi would approach the Indian Army, the possibility of a last, all-out slaughter of civilians by Pakistani troops—all were subjects of speculation. Rumours proliferated in Delhi as, doubtless, everywhere. The speed with which they were transmitted was almost as astonishing as their variety—a broad spectrum ranging from fact to fancy.

The average Indian, however, is fortunate in his easy access to a large number of uncensored newspapers, both Indian and international magazines and radio; and the Indian and foreign journalists accompanying the Army's advance towards Dacca quickly filed their stories. Thus some of the more absurd rumours were soon discredited (though some of the more blatantly sensational ones appear, with the disclosure of the Anderson papers, to have been quite true).

However, despite the mass of high level media coverage of events, it was still difficult, reading different articles written by different correspondents, printed in different papers, to gain an accurate picture of the delirium and drama taking place in Dacca. This, then, is an attempt to present a cohesive account of the surrender story.

On the morning of Friday, 17 December, headlines announced what had been known to almost everyone since the previous evening—that at 4.31 pm on Thursday afternoon Niazi had signed the Instrument of Surrender and the war (in Bangla Desh at any rate) was over. This, in fact, was not a sudden and miraculous event. It represented the culmination of 24 hours of intense backstage manoeuvres, high level cables and messages and, for those directly involved, pressures of excitement, anticipation and uncertainty.

It appears that on the afternoon of 14 December a message from Niazi had come through to the American Embassy in New Delhi offering his surrender and that of the forces under his command in Bangla Desh. The offer was not unconditional but the few qualifications were largely of a face-saving nature and since time, rather than the ultimate outcome, was the issue, they posed no stumbling blocks.

This message was immediately relayed to Washington where, after reaching Secretary of State Rogers' desk, it was conveyed to the White House. From the White House came back word that a surrender by Niazi without the knowledge and permission of his Commander-in-Chief, Yahya Khan, was unacceptable; at any rate the American government was not going to have anything to do with it. By this time, evening was well advanced, as top level communications channels were mobilised and a frantic effort was made to get through to Yahya. While contact with high echelons of the Pakistan government was fairly and quickly established, the President and Commander-in-Chief, in this supreme moment of national crisis, was not communicable. Attempts to consult Yahya beginning at 11.00 pm on the evening of the 15th, were unavailing until the early hours of the following morning.

When Yahya surfaced and his authorisation for Niazi's surrender obtained, the American Embassy so informed

Indian Army Headquarters. However, it is reported that General Manekshaw had, in the interim, already received a message through United Nations channels telling him to expect a momentary announcement of surrender (indicating perhaps, that Pakistani envoys to the UN had alerted the Security Council).

In Dacca, meanwhile, excitement and tension, already high, were mounting to a super-pitch. Niazi's gesture on the morning of 15 December, of suing for a ceasefire and withdrawal of his troops to agreed areas for subsequent repatriation to Pakistan, reflected what everyone in Dacca know— that Indian forces were about to enter the city. Would Niazi bow to the inevitable or would he honour his promise to "fight to the last"? The latter course would entail a further massive cost in lives to a populace which had already suffered almost beyond belief.

General Manekshaw, after informing Niazi that a ceasefire was unacceptable, again urged surrender and ordered a halt of the bombing of Dacca—between 5.00 pm on the afternoon of 15 December and (in the absence of further agreement) 9.00 am the following morning.

In the Intercontinental Hotel in Dacca, scene of so much vivid Bangla Desh reporting the previous March, there was an air of last-moment apprehension. Among other occupants of the hotel were the Governor, Mr Malik, members of his former cabinet and their families. The emotional manifestation of apprehensions by some of the wives did not detract from the theatrical aspects of the moment. Some reporters speculated whether, despite the horrors of the past nine months, the people of East Bengal were really committed to the concept of a sovereign Bangla Desh. Assuming that they were, might not the achievement of a sovereignty so vastly dependent upon India's support spawn its own set of problems from the outset? These doubts were soon to be resolved.

The conditions that Niazi had stipulated in his last message to General Manekshaw were: guarantee of safety for all military and para-military forces, safety of all those settled in

"East Pakistan" since 1947 and no reprisals against those who had helped the administration since March 1971. He was pleading for the butchers: but the Indians were adamant— the surrender must be according to international code as laid down in the Geneva Convention. General Manekshaw had already pledged his words, with full confidence, that his Army would adhere to that code.

By then, Major-General Jamshed, GOC of 36 Pak Division, had packed in and given himself up, together with as many of his troops as he still controlled, to the Indian army.

At 1.00 pm, Major-General Jacob, General Aurora's Chief of Staff, was flown into Dacca by helicopter with a draft Instrument of Surrender. At 3.00 pm General Nagra entered Dacca city from the north-west with four battalions while news was received from Magura that Major-General Ansari, GOC 9 Pak Division, had surrendered with his forces.

General Niazi accepted and initiated the draft Instrument of Surrender.

General Aurora, accompanied by Air Marshal Dewan (Air Officer Commanding-in-Chief, East) Vice-Admiral Krishnan (Flag Officer Commanding-in-Chief, East) and Group Captain Khondakar (Chief of Staff of Bangla Desh's Mukti Bahini High Command) flew to Dacca to receive the surrender.

The Instrument of Surrender was signed at 4.31 pm at Dacca Racecourse.

Much has been written describing the events at the Racecourse that afternoon. It was appropriate that the ceremony of surrender was held at the scene of Sheikh Mujib's famous address nine months earlier. Bangla Desh had survived a turbulent gestation—and was reborn that day.

Dacca went wild with joy. The nearly mad euphoria of the crowd was a catharsis of months of fear and horror. Some of the scenes, as the citizens of Bangla Desh celebrated their independence and hailed the Indian troops' entry into Dacca, must have bordered on the comical. It is difficult to visualise General Aurora being hoisted to the shoulders of the crowd and carried from the Racecourse in this unusual mode of transport for a senior officer—or General Nagra standing on the hood of his jeep joining in the crowd's jubilant chanting of "Joi Bangla". It is delightful to contemplate the idea of burly, turbanned Sikhs being hugged, kissed and profusely garlanded by Bengalis; and tough Gorkhas, receiving the same treatment, marching along with flowers heaped on their hats and decorating the barrels of their rifles. Flowers cascaded from rooftops on to the dancing crowds below. If happiness can be measured in tons of expended marigolds, Dacca must, that day, have been the happiest and most auspicious city in history.

CHAPTER IX

The War in the Air and at Sea

In war, it is the troops who move by land—who conquer territories, occupy enemy positions and take the enemy prisoner—on whom the limelight focuses. Theirs is the tangible achievement and it is their success or failure that affects the day-to-day lives of human beings. The contribution made by those who fight in the air or at sea—however crucial—affects the ordinary man only at one remove. Their heroism is acknowledged and rewarded but their activities remain remote. It is the task of the historian to interpret their achievements in terms of a more personal involvement.

The 1971 war was essentially an all-arms war. This strategically necessary requirement was fulfilled for two main reasons: the government gave the Armed Forces a clear-cut aim; and, from the first, the Chiefs of Staff, the Manekshaw-Lal-Nanda team, worked in unison and in a spirit of co-operation that filtered all the way down to the units.

The role of the air arm in war is two fold—strategic and tactical. In the strategic role the air force operates, within the general charter of the overall political aim, on long-range tasks where its successes or failures are not immediately discernible—such as strategic bombing of enemy industries, ports and other communications complexes, fuel plants and storages, and similar targets. Also, since its responsibility is to defend its own country against the enemy's air forces, it must strive to gain superiority in the air—general and local. These are vital tasks and take priority over tactical roles such as interdiction and close support of land and naval forces.

There are occasions when too much emphasis is placed on the strategic role—to the detriment of tactical support. In the Second World War, for instance, whereas the Russians used their air forces primarily in support of surface operations, the Allies—particularly during the early years of the war—laid overwhelming stress on the strategic role, with the result that forces operating by land did not receive adequate close air support. It was not until the Second Front in Europe was opened that General Eisenhower was able to prevail on the "Bomber Barons" to de-emphasise the strategic role. The RAF and USAAF in North-west Europe were consequently able to give full support to 21 Army Group.

In India also there has been a conflict of priorities regarding the role of the air arm: in the 1965 operations one of the Army's complaints, particularly during the first few days, was that it seldom saw the Air Force in evidence. In this war the Air Chief was determined that, regardless of the demands for strategic tasks, a proportion of air effort would be allotted for the ground support role on both the western and eastern fronts from the very beginning of operations.

On the western front, where it was presumed that the Pakistanis would take the initiative, a pre-emptive strike by the PAF was expected. The Air Chief made his plans to disperse his squadrons and at the same time activated his forward airbases in readiness for a counter-strike.

Pakistan's air-strike force was appreciably stronger, with more sophisticated aircraft, than in 1965. Besides the *F-104A Starfighters* it already possessed, it had acquired *MIG-19s* from the Chinese and *Mirage IIIEs* from France and its total strength had grown to 265 front line aircraft. Whereas the *MIG-19* is qualitatively inferior to the IAF's *MIG-21*, the sophisticated *Mirage,* with its (US manufactured) infra-red sensor equipment for night fighting and its greater capability at low level warfare, is superior to anything the IAF has.

With this air-power, and given the advantages of initiative and surprise, the PAF might well have succeeded in making a dent in India's air power if it had planned and executed its pre-emptive strike efficiently. In the event, however, the PAF strike turned out to be a damp squib. It was ill-conceived and timidly executed. Instead of an early-morning first strike, which would have given the PAF the whole day to keep pounding at the airfields, the pre-emptive bid was made at dusk, thus giving the Indian Engineers all night to repair the little damage that was caused. Secondly, the air-strike was launched on too timid a scale. With the exception of a bid for Agra, there was no attack in depth. Nor was the offensive carried out in strength: flights of only three or four aircrafts attacked a few forward airfields. The long range capacity of the *Mirage* was not utilised. Throughout the war it was the same—there was hardly any attempt to penetrate beyond the Amritsar-Pathankot line although the *Mirage* has the capacity to bomb targets as far afield as New Delhi and Lucknow.

The IAF's Intelligence system—based on radar air surveillance equipment as well as the recently deployed observer posts equipped with VHF sets—gave it adequate warning of approaching enemy aircraft. Unlike 1965, no airbase was caught unawares: even in the first pre-emptive strike the PAF failed to destroy a single IAF aircraft on the ground.

There has been some comment about the ease with which the PAF seemed to penetrate Indian air space on the first night—and the delay in retaliation by the IAF. What was remarkable, in fact, was the relatively brief time-lag between the surprise attack of the enemy and the IAF's counter-strike. Since the actual date and time the PAF would launch its surprise attack could not be known, Indian aircraft had been dispersed and pulled out of range. It was only after the opening act of war that Indian fighters and bombers could bomb-up and take to wing from forward bases. The first bomber was over Pakistan at 11.00 pm—a remarkable feat considering that it takes four hours to bomb-up a *Canberra*. The targets attacked on the first night included airfields at Chander, Sargodha, Masrur, Risalwala, Chaklala and Murid, as well as radar stations at Sakesar and Bidan. Until 5.00 am the following morning, 4 December, bombers and fighter bombers attacked targets flying singly.

That the IAF's counter-strike was effective was proved by the sudden decline in the enemy's air effort after the first day. It appeared that the back of the PAF had been broken after the first 24 hours. While its aircraft cohtinued to make hit-and-run raids over Indian airbases and to give close support to the Pak land forces—particularly in the Chhamb offensive— air superiority was established by India from the very first day and never, thereafter, seriously challenged. The extent of the PAF's incapacitation can be gauged by the fact that there was no attempt to attack the Indian Navy's Task Force when, on 5 December, it made its bold foray off Karachi where its own air cover—at that range—was most tenuous. It was the same in the Rajasthan sector at the Longanewala offensive. Indian *HF-24s* kept attacking and destroying Pak tanks for several hours: no PAF aircraft appeared to challenge the Indian planes.

It is now thought that the damage caused by the IAF counter-strike on the first night of the war was probably much more effective than first reports indicated. It is likely that as many as 30 enemy aircrafts may have been destroyed or damaged on the night of 3/4 December. Certainly the radar station at Sakesar, a vital link in Pakistan's air surveillance system, was seriously damaged. Even at the end of the war it had not been fully repaired.

The meticulous "claims" procedure at IAF Headquarters— whereby only certain kills, supported by photographic evidence, were counted—ensured that no optimistic or misleading assessments were entertained. Every claim was evaluated on its evidential merits by a special board at Air Headquarters before it was allowed to be announced to the press—a procedure greatly different from that which prevailed in 1965.

Strategic targets included the Karachi port complex and the oil storage tanks. The latter burned for eight days. The first attack against the Karachi oil tanks was made by a flight of four *Hunters* coming in low from the sea-ward side skimming the surface of the water. The Karachi anti-aircraft defences were the most formidable of any in Pakistan, but the *Hunters* scored direct hits, destroying millions of gallons of precious fuel. The Sui gas works were also put out of action. As a result of these attacks the Pakistani fuel reserves were considerably reduced.

As regards ground support, strategic operations were not allowed to interfere with the sorties required for close support of land forces. The air strike at Longanewala is now a familiar story—as is the successful tank-destroying mission of the IAF over Chhamb—where several IAF aircraft were destroyed or damaged by ground fire in the incessant daily strikes. The strikes, both accurate and successful, claimed a large number of kills.

An important aspect of the air plan was maritime reconnaissance. The main bases for these operations were on the Andaman Islands, Chaubatia (in Orissa), Vishakhapatnam and Madras on the east coast. Cochin, Goa, Bombay and Oakha were the pivotal points in the west. Unlike 1965, the air reconnaissance cover over these waters prevented any surprise moves by the enemy against our ports and coastal installations.

The air war in the east has already been described. The enemy air force ceased to be effective after the second day of the war. Thereafter the IAF had absolute mastery of the air and this was one of the greatest contributory factors to the fast rate of movement on land.

The Air Force averaged 500 sorties per day—the largest air effort since the Second World War. Even then, the IAF capacity was never utilised to the full (about 1,500 sorties per day if stretched to the maximum).

This tremendous and sustained air effort could be maintained because of the high rate of serviceability attained by the ground staff. One of the changes that Air Chief Marshal Lal had brought about when he assumed his appointment was the integration of the technical and equipment branches of the IAF, and it paid dividends in the maintenance standards of Indian aircraft throughout the war.

Considerably surprise was caused by the reluctance of PAF pilots to take on their Indian counterparts in aerial combat. Even their attempts to bomb Indian airfields displayed a lack of determination: they would drop their bombs at the first opportunity, jettison their tanks and turn back for home. As one senior IAF officer remarked, "It has been a terrible disgrace to the machines they were handling." In contrast, the combat conduct of Indian pilots surpassed all previous achievements. Some pilots were able to make as many as five sorties a day—and the general complaint was that they were never engaged by the enemy.

Decisive as the air victory was, it must be remembered that the Indian Air Force, like the Indian Army, enjoyed a marked degree of numerical superiority over the Pakistanis. That both Services also achieved qualitative superiority reflects the high state of equipment, training and morale of the two Services during recent years.

The Indian Navy was the one Service which did not enjoy material superiority over its enemy. By and large its ships were older and less manoeuvrable than those of the Pakistan Navy. In a fleet action at sea the Indian Navy would have been out-manoeuvred and probably out-gunned. It is to the great credit of the Naval Chief and his admirals that, instead of waiting to be confronted by the enemy fleet, the Indian Navy boldly sailed out to seek battle under conditions of its own choosing and, in one daring and spectacular attack, destroyed Pakistan's power to wage war at sea.

This was the first war in which the naval arm of the Indian Armed Forces played a key, operational role—and it was played with great *panache*. It was the Indian Navy's debut—and the setting was as grand as the success complete.

The military concept in India has always been continental—with strategy focused on land warfare, fought at varying degrees of intensity, escalation and involvement of the other two Services. In the 1947-48 Kashmir war the campaign was mainly confined to ground operations with a minimum commitment of the Air Force. There were no sweeps by Indian squadrons to gain air superiority. The fledgling PAF stayed out of battle. The 1961 Goa campaign was indeed an all-Services operation but on a minor scale: in any case, the main effort of the Navy was confined to territorial waters. In 1962, the war against the Chinese never escalated to include combat aircraft or naval equipment. In 1965 the air arm played a crucial role in full-scale air operations but the war itself remained land locked. Although movement of Pakistani merchant ships was brought to a standstill, the Navy did not come into its own in any spectacular way.

The general impression on the public, and one not dispelled by pronouncements even by senior army generals regarding the relative unimportance of the naval arm in India's security, was that the Indian Navy was a minor Service largely maintained for reasons of pomp and prestige. The Silent Service suffered this aspersion quietly for twenty-five years—and suffered in other ways as well. It was never in the forefront when allotments were made by the Ministry and it is only in very recent times that it has been given a reasonable priority in the Defence Services re-equipment and modernisation programme.

The fact is that deployment of the naval arm to its full potential has international implications. Unlike the Army and the Air Force which operate on or over home territory or the territory of the immediate belligerents, the Navy, at full steam so to say, must break out of territorial waters and operate on the open seas. This is a form of escalation in which the super-powers may indulge—as, indeed, they frequently do. It is not a game that smaller powers can play without inviting complications. Until 1971 India had not taken recourse to this step.

During the 1971 war, the Navy's role on the open seas was of crucial importance and the game was played with consummate finesse.

The isolation of Bangla Desh from Pakistani (or pro-Pakistani) intervention entailed "contraband control and blockade" as envisaged in international maritime law. It also required

the isolation of both Bangla Desh and Pakistan and the closure
of their ports to all foreign ships. It meant conducting naval
operations which would remain confined to action against
enemy vessels only and would not escalate into unrestricted
trade warfare. Great powers can afford over-reaction to ensure total blockade. India, particularly in view of the climate
of international opinion that then existed, could not. The
Indian Navy was required to achieve its aim of complete
isolation of Pakistan's and Bangla Desh's ports but it trod
a delicate line of international opinion. It fulfilled all the
requirements—in its very first naval war.

The crucial task of the Indian Navy on the outbreak of
war was not only to isolate the enemy's ports but also to
keep India's sea routes open and to keep her own ships plying.
The facts record its success: not one ship was able to bring
supplies or war materials to Pakistan or its occupation government in the east; in the process it sank a large part of the enemy
fleet while avoiding all confrontation on an international scale;
it kept all Indian sea-lanes open—enabling 130 ships to sail
unscathed into home ports during the 14-day war. (At one
time there were 44 Indian ships in the Arabian Sea and the
Bay of Bengal). It established world-wide control over Indian
shipping by co-ordinating its routing and programming to
provide maximum security.

The major re-organisation that had taken place in the Indian
Navy since the 1965 war was that it now contained two naval
commands—as well as the Southern Naval Area at Cochin.
Western Naval Command was located at Bombay and Eastern
Naval Command at Vishakhapatnam.

The threats posed by the Pakistani Navy were:

1. Bombardment of coastal targets, particularly the
   threatened stretch along the Saurashtra coast;
2. Submarine and surface threat to Indian shipping and
   warships at sea;
3. Sabotage and clandestine attacks on harbour installations
   and on ships in harbour.

Of particular danger were the *Midget* and *Chariot* submarines which Pakistan had recently acquired. The *Midget*
is a small submarine crewed by eight to ten men, with a sufficient long-range capacity to enable an attack on Bombay
from a base in Karachi. The *Chariot* is less a submarine (in
the conventional sense) than a human-controlled torpedo
which must be launched near the target. It is guided against
an enemy ship with a delayed-action fuse. The Pakistan Navy
was also known to have trained a Special Service Group in
frogmen operations and the use of limpet mines.

The tasks given by the Naval Chief to the Fleet were:
1. The destruction of Pakistan's Naval forces;
2. The capture or destruction of Pakistani merchant
    vessels;
3. The safety of Indian merchant ships at sea and the naval
    control of all shipping;
4. Safeguarding against:
    (a) threat of naval bombardment;
    (b) sabotage and clandestine attacks;
5. Contraband control;
6. The isolation of Bangla Desh and the port of Karachi.

Since the bulk of the surface ships of the Pakistani Navy
was known to be in Karachi, the first task—destruction of
Pak naval forces—became the responsibility of Vice-Admiral
S.N. Kohli, FOC-in-C Western Naval Command. Shortly
after war was declared, a composite Task Force (which included
a number of newly acquired Russian rocket boats) sailed out
of Indian waters on its mission.

The Pakistani Naval force in Karachi was formidable—
seven powerful, modernised destroyers, a 6,000-ton light
cruiser and a number of supporting ships. Two submarines
were known to be operating in the Arabian Sea.

Karachi was a heavily defended port. There were several
fighter squadrons based on the neighbouring airfields for
the air defence of the city and the harbour complex. On the

sea-ward side there were rings of radar sets deployed to give early warning of approaching ships and aircraft—and sophisticated radar-controlled guns and missiles to thicken up the anti-aircraft cover.

The Indian Task Force planned to approach the Karachi coastline by night, though this was likely to create difficulties about distinguishing between enemy and neutral shipping. However, in the event this problem was resolved by the Pakistanis themselves, who issued an order forbidding foreign ships from approaching within 75 miles of Karachi at night.

Maintaining radio silence, the Task Force arrived off Karachi at midnight on 4/5 December. Its radar screen soon picked up four echoes, two of which indicated fast-moving warships—and the Indian Navy opened fire. Thus was the battle started and the result was the destruction of two destroyers, the *Khaiber* and the *Shahjehan,* two mine-sweepers and three other ships.

After the naval battle the Task Force further surprised the enemy by taking an even bolder step. Although the Commander of the Force still expected an attack by the PAF, rather than retire to base he steamed his Force closer into shore and began bombardment of the port, inflicting heavy damage on the harbour and its oil installations.

Not content with the success achieved in this first attack, Western Naval Command sent out another Task Force four days later to carry out yet another daring raid. This time one unit of the Force attacked Karachi while a second engaged military targets on the Makran coast west of Karachi, right up to the Iranian border, paying special attention to Gwadar, Pakistan's second largest port. Three more enemy ships were damaged by the Indian Navy in its raid on Karachi and the fuel tank farm was set alight.

Unfortunately, the anti-submarine frigate, the *Khukri,* which had stayed behind to cover the withdrawal of the Task Force was sunk by an enemy submarine.

In the Bay of Bengal, the main task was to deny supplies to the occupation government in Bangla Desh and to prevent any enemy forces from escaping. The main unit in these waters was the aircraft carrier *Vikrant,* supported by a destroyer, frigates and submarines.

Long before the commencement of hostilities, the FOC-in-C, anticipating the Pakistani Navy's attempt to send in submarines to destroy Indian warships in a surprise raid, had sent the *Vikrant* out to sea off the northern end of the Andaman Islands. Events justified this cautionary measure: the American submarine *Diablo* (loaned to Pakistan without Congressional sanction and re-named *Ghazi* by the PN) was sunk in Vizag harbour.

As soon as Pakistan declared war, the Eastern Fleet went into action. By 10.30 am on 4 December the *Vikrant* sent out her first flight of *Sea Hawks* to bomb Cox's Bazar, putting the airfield out of action. Steaming north, the *Vikrant* was within bombing range of Chittagong by early afternoon. Her aircraft attacked both the harbour and the airfield.

On or about 9 December, reports were received at General Aurora's Eastern Command Headquarters that enemy groups were escaping by the overland route through Cox's Bazar to Burma. In order to cut off their escape route it was necessary to land a small force at Cox's Bazar.

Unfortunately, the only Landing Ship (LST) then available was out to sea. Nothing daunted, the FOC-in-C decided to transport the force by merchant ship and transfer it to the LST on the high seas—a bold decision. A battalion and a half were hastily pulled out of battle from the Jessore front and put aboard the *S.S. Vishwavijaya,* an Indian merchant vessel of approximately 6,000-tons which then happened to be anchored in the Hoogly. The *Vishwavijaya* took the force to a point off the Cox's Bazar coast where the transfer took place. This was the first "combined operations" landing ever made by the Indian armed forces.

"Contraband control" and the isolation of Bangla Desh and Karachi remained the major tasks of the Indian Navy. In their execution the Navy inspected more than 115 neutral ships (relying heavily on Southern Naval Command based at Cochin). It also captured three Pakistani merchant ships.

The only *contretemps* with serious international potential was brought about by President Nixon's gratuitous attempt at escalation by sending a task force from the United States Seventh Fleet steaming towards the Bay of Bengal from the Indo-China theatre. This formidable force consisted of the nuclear-powered aircraft-carrier *Enterprise* (capable of launching *Phantom* aircraft armed with nuclear warheads) the Commando Carrier (Amphibious Attack Ship), the *Tripoli*, a guided missile frigate, a number of destroyers, dock-landing ships and supply ships. The purpose of this deployment was not then disclosed but the White House explanation that this substantial force was sent to facilitate the evacuation of the few Americans left in Bangla Desh (for the most part missionaries who had chosen of their own accord to remain in Bangla Desh) convinced no one. Fortunately, before the Task Force could move deep into the Bay of Bengal, the lightning campaign was over and it edged away towards the southern waters off the Maldive Islands.

CHAPTER X

Commentary on the Campaign

The campaign that the Indian Chiefs of Staff conducted for the liberation of Bangla Desh was a great achievement by any standards. The firm and confident political handling of the problem by Mrs Gandhi and her government was matched by the sophisticated management, direction and leadership of the Indian armed forces. It is only now, after the successful conclusion of the lightning campaign in the east, that the difference between this and other wars that India has fought before becomes clearly discernible.

Firstly, there was a clear political aim—something that the Service Chiefs have not always received in the past. It is apparent that the possibility of having to invade Bangla Desh in support of the liberation forces of that country had been foreseen for some time. In spite of the Indian reluctance to be the first to aggress, Mrs Gandhi firmly retained the initiative for military action in the east and played the game of conflict-control with consummate skill to gain advantage in the border confrontation in Bangla Desh. It was the crassness of the second-rate generals who controlled Pakistan politically and militarily that provided the opportunity that India sought.

The political aims given to the Indian Chiefs of Staff, clearly, were:

To liberate Bangla Desh as quickly as possible;
To fight a holding action in the west and in the north, if attacked;

To make limited gains in the west, as a bargaining point
in case a Pakistani surprise attack succeeded in capturing
any part of Indian territory.

Despite much accusation to the contrary—particularly
from Washington—it is obvious that there was never any
intent to strike deep into Pakistani territory in the west. This
becomes apparent from the conduct of the defensive battle
fought by India: the main strategic reserve, the powerful
1st Armoured Division with supporting infantry divisions,
was never committed. It is important to emphasise this at
the start, not necessarily to refute charges levelled by hostile
governments abroad, but because even in India there are
chauvinistic elements who, judging from pronouncements
already made, might insidiously create the myth that the
armed forces would have made sensational conquests had
Mrs Gandhi not ordered a unilateral ceasefire. There was never
any intention to assail the integrity of the state of West Pakistan. India desired only to liberate Bangla Desh because there
was no other way—after nine months of frustration in diplomatic endeavour—to solve the problem of Pakistan's intolerable
and steadily mounting demographic aggression.

The military task before the Indian Chiefs of Staff was to
manipulate the balance of forces which were designed to combat a dual threat in such a way that a third, uncatered-for,
military problem could be solved without compromising the
country's security. The crucial factor, of course, would be
time: the third task must be completed before major threats
could develop on the other two fronts.

We have seen how the balance of forces was manipulated.
Taking a calculated risk, a number of army and air formations
were diverted from the northern and western fronts to provide a
minimum degree of superiority needed for Eastern Command to
enable it to complete its task. The speed with which this could
be done was the crucial issue—and it would depend upon
a number of factors, the first among which was the degree
of cooperation between the three Services. The flexibility and

the improvisation that marked the Bangla Desh campaign was a direct result of this inter-Service cooperation.

Assessments of the length of time that the Pakistani occupation forces could hold out varied from two months to two weeks. Niazi had stocked up the Pak strongholds for two months: the American Chiefs of Staff estimated three to four weeks: Yahya Khan was sure that it would be long enough for some form of intervention, the Chinese Army in Tibet or the US Seventh Fleet, or whatever, to prevent a defeat. The high command in Delhi banked on a sufficient rate of progress to be able to start pulling out army and air formations, to re-inforce the other two fronts, by about the tenth day: and in the event it was able to do even better.

It was not the victory that was so remarkable: there could never have been any doubt about that. The Chiefs of Staff had placed sufficient forces at the disposal of the Army Commander in Calcutta to ensure that he would take Dacca. By dividing his army in the two wings, Yahya Khan had placed his forces at a strategic disadvantage: and what tactical advantages the terrain in Bangla Desh offered him, he and his generals were too witless to exploit. As regards relative strengths, though General Aurora had only a tenuous superiority (7 to 4) he had the initiative—and that enables a commander to achieve the requisite superiority at points of his own choosing.

What *was* remarkable was the incredible speed with which his forces moved across a country which is, in effect, a vast alluvial delta criss-crossed by a thousand rivers, rivulets, canals and creeks—particularly in the eastern and western sectors. When the story of the conduct of operations can be told in all its detail, military history will have acquired a new dimension in improvised, dynamic movement—both in tactical and logistical execution.

That Eastern Command was able to beat the deadline reflects not only on General Aurora's bold and imaginative plan and the dash and determination with which his corps and divisional commanders carried it out but also on the intimate support he received from the IAF and IN. Close air support, helicopter operations for "air-bridging", landings from the sea—whatever support he required from the two other Services he received in full measure, and not always preplanned.

Another contribution to the mobility of the operations was the enthusiastic support given by the Mukti Bahini. In the aftermath of regular operations of this kind the contribution made by irregular forces is often underplayed. To do so would, in this instance, be singularly invidious because the support and cooperation supplied by the guerillas was remarkable. Those elements of the Bahini trained and equipped to fight as regular infantry were, in view of the short preparatory period, not as operationally significant as the vast number of guerilla groups that acted as eyes and ears for the advancing forces.

One of the major disadvantages from which India has suffered in previous wars and confrontations is insufficient Intelligence. There was no such drawback in this war. With 75 million people on its side, civil and military Intelligence had access to virtually any information it required—both tactical and strategic, before and during the campaign. The highly educated personnel of the Mukti Bahini readily understood what information was required, where and how to get it, and how and when it should be conveyed for maximum utility and effectiveness. Indian forces from the earliest days of confrontation on the border were almost invariably in possession of detailed information regarding enemy locations, moves and even intentions. One of the reasons why the swift by-passing moves during the campaign were so effective was that within a few hours of hitting against an enemy position, local volunteers would carry out a quick reconnaissance at great risk to themselves, return with the necessary information and then act as guides if needed.

As regards long-range Intelligence cover, Intelligence channels, once organised, provided a steady flow of reliable information from Dacca and other centres. This was the first war in which India has had to rely solely on her own Intelligence resources as far as "mechanical" cover is concerned. However, her wireless intercept service has now achieved a sophisticated level of electronic know-how and, on the eastern front, India was not only able to gather factual and political Intelligence but, in some cases, plans and projections of the enemy high command. Further, once the Indians had broken the Pakistani code, India was able to conduct an Intelligence "offensive" against the enemy; that is, to force the enemy, by a combination of psychological warfare and deception, to adopt a course of action beneficial to Indian interests. Forcing Dr Malik to resign was one example of the success of this Intelligence offensive; persuading Niazi to abandon the defence of Dacca, another.

Prohibiting the enemy's access to useful Intelligence is perhaps as important as obtaining information of enemy locations and movement. In this also, the Indian forces in Bangla Desh enjoyed a tremendous advantage: as no Bengali would act as an informer for the hated Pakistani, there was virtually no fifth column. Whatever information was needed by occupation forces they had to get for themselves; and the resistances forces ensured that Pakistani patrols were minimal both in frequency and effectiveness. Senior commanders among the Pakistani prisoners of war have since confirmed that the Mukti Bahini guerillas so controlled the countryside that very little night movement could be undertaken outside the cantonments and fortresses. In most areas only daytime patrols were carried out—and then only in large bodies. Consequently, the Pakistanis seldom had information concerning Indian attacks or by-passing moves.

The role played by the Border Security Forces in this war, far greater in scope than any envisaged at the time of its inception, has been duly recognised by the Prime Minister and the Army Chief. In the early days of the Bangla Desh crisis the BSF was entrusted with the responsibility of assisting and supporting members of the liberation forces who had escaped to Indian sanctuaries or were operating from the border regions. This task was greatly facilitated by the fact that the BSF and the EPR, until recently deployed against each other, were in fairly close contact even before the onset of the crisis. However, the manner in which this force was able quickly to assess the situation and take the initiative in border confrontations deserves credit. During those early days the BSF rendered yeoman service in the collection and evaluation of intelligence of events inside Bangla Desh.

The BSF bore almost sole responsibility for border operations until Army formations could be made available for deployment in Eastern Command. Even after the Army moved in, the BSF continued to play a significant role—in many instances bearing the brunt of enemy armour and artillery onslaughts. When the offensive began, units of the BSF moved in with Indian forces in operational roles. Their casualties, 600 dead, wounded and missing correspond, in proportion to their total strength, with casualty figures for the Army.

A refreshing aspect of the war was the smooth handling of the press—particularly on the eastern front. Even before the war started, when there might have been justifiable security reasons for keeping the press at a distance, Government of India allowed both foreign and Indian correspondents access to the Bangla Desh border—and many availed of the opportunity to go into Bangla Desh to report on Mukti Bahini operations. The confidence placed in the press paid worthwhile dividends. From the beginning millions of people all over the world were kept in touch with the endeavours of the freedom fighters and sympathy for their aims, aspirations and achievements became world-wide.

During the war, the Ministry of Defence co-opted the services of a General Officer to be its spokesman at briefings for the press—with the result that news coverage of the operations, unlike in previous wars, was knowledgeable, competent and objective. Foreign and Indian war correspondents accompanied leading troops during the invasion—so that the impact of the spectacular successes were graphically portrayed day-by-day in the world's press.

For the first time, foreign correspondents were able to see

the Indian Armed Forces in action for prolonged periods. This, as much as anything else, re-established the image of the Indian fighting man as a disciplined professional, cool and determined in battle, proud of his Service—and with full confidence in his immediate superior officers and in the generals who directed their operations.

Sidney Schanberg of the *New York Times,* who accompanied the troops successively in two sectors, has nothing but the highest praise for the officers and men he saw in action. A young, intelligent, articulate American of the liberal generation that does not take kindly to war and violence, his impressions—as nearly in his own words as memory can recall— had this to say of Indian troops:

> I don't like sitting around praising armies. I don't like armies because armies mean war—and I don't like wars. But this (the Indian) army was something.... They were great all the way. There was never a black mark.... I lived with the officers and I walked, rode with the jawans— and they were all great.... Sure some of them were scared at first—they wouldn't be human if they weren't. But I never saw a man flinch because he was scared. There is a tremendous spirit (in the Indian Army) and it did one good to experience it.... I have seen our boys in Vietnam—· and this army was different. Their (the Indian Army's) arms and equipment aren't as good—but what they had they used with effect.... and could they improvise! I saw recoilless guns carried on shoulders, big guns pushed across marshes like ox-carts, by jawans, villagers, officers; everybody was in it together.... And they were the most perfect gentlemen—I never saw them do a wrong thing—not even when they saw just how bestial the enemy had been.

The people of Bangla Desh will talk of the Indian Army with affection and gratitude for many years—of their feats in battle, their humanity, their courage and determination— just as the Indian Army, who have such good reason to be grateful for the wholehearted support of a cruelly treated but courageous people, will remember for long the bonds that have been established between the Indian and the Bangla Deshi.

Finally, the historic perspective: India, with no support from the democratic governments of the Western world—

and in the face of active hostility from one—boldly committed herself to the establishment of an independent Bangla Desh. Mrs Gandhi was clear and determined about this policy from the start—and over the months she converted her colleagues and advisers to it also: and when diplomatic approaches brought no response from any corner of the world, she resorted to the only course open—military action. In the years to come, when Golden Bengal builds itself up into a smiling nation, history will surely grant her the accolade that the contemporary world withheld—and perhaps repeat the poet Southey's description of Blenheim:

" 'T WAS A FAMOUS VICTORY"

Postscript

The battle had been won. Bangla Desh had succeeded in her bid for independence but the elation of victory was lacking in one respect: Sheikh Mujib, the Bangapita, was still in prison, his fate still controlled by the defeated power. It occurred to many that the absolute quality of the Pakistani defeat in Bangla Desh might unleash the *jehad* spirit and further jeopardise the Sheikh's safety. It would appear that this was a valid concern. Aware that his downfall was imminent, one of Yahya's last acts in power was to order Mujib's execution. A story that will probably never be confirmed and may well be apocryphal is that Z.A. Bhutto's reaction to this proposition was: "Come off it, Ivan the Terrible. You've done enough damage as it is."

Despite Bhutto's first presidential message which was hardly conciliatory towards India, the new President apparently realised the senselessness of continuing the vendetta against Mujib. At the time of the ceasefire a near-universal assumption had been that the Sheikh's freedom, and possibly his life, would be a Pakistani trump card in negotiations for the repatriation of prisoners of war. It is interesting to speculate what motives, other than a last-ditch effort to re-establish ties with Bangla Desh led Bhutto, a shrewd politician, to make this gratuitous though equitable gesture.

President Bhutto's intention of releasing the Sheikh was made public at a mass rally where he skilfully solicited the crowd's approval of this course. In Dacca, of course, the news was received with rapturous acclaim by crowds already nearly surfeited with emotion. The mystery surrounding the date of the release, Mr. Bhutto's secret (a neat piece of showmanship), added a mildly nerve-wracking element to the situation.

The news of Mujib's arrival in London on 8 January was hailed with elation and relief around the world. While the timing had been anticipated by many, the location was a surprise. It was in fact a brilliant choice of a reasonably neutral milieu and, in view of the British role in the original partition of the sub-continent, one not un-mixed with historic irony. Certainly the leader of Bangla Desh was received handsomely by his hosts. He was extended all *protocolaire* courtesies, invited to confer with Prime Minister Heath and, on his departure, offered an RAF jet to convey him to Delhi.

During his short stop-over in Delhi the Sheikh was, of course, accorded the highest honours due to a visiting Head of State. The solidarity of purpose and friendship between the two nations was much stressed. While Mujib gratefully acknowledged Bangla Desh's debt to India, Mrs Gandhi expressed satisfaction that she had been able to achieve her three aims in relation to the liberation of Bangla Desh: to send the refugees back; to help the Mukti Bahini; and to secure the Sheikh's release.

The real delirium of welcome was, however, reserved for Dacca where motions ran high on both public and personal levels. For many, this must have been the moment when the struggle for independence was finally over. With the Bangapita's appearance before the vast crowd at the Dacca Racecourse, scene both of his famous address ten months earlier and of General Niazi's surrender, history completed a neat circle.

APPENDIX 'A'

Arms Aid to Pakistan

UNITED STATES

Under the Military Assistance Programme, the United States undertook to equip a force of 5½ to 6 divisions of the Pakistani Army with modern equipment and also to train them. It supplied, mainly:

Modern infantry weapons, including semi-automatic rifles, carbines, light and medium machine-guns, infantry mortars, recoilless rifles of 57 and 106 mm calibre and 105 mm and 155 mm howitzers.

300 Armoured Personnel Carriers

200 *Sherman,* 250 *Chaffee,* about 100 *M-41 Bulldog* and 460 *M-47/M-48 Patton* tanks.

Full complement of engineering, transport and signal equipment.

Ammunition, including sophisticated Variable Time Electronic Fuses, to fight a two-month war.

AIR FORCE

10 *Lockkeed T-33 A* Trainers
7 *Lockheed RT-33A* Reconnaissance-Trainers
120 *F-86 Sabre* Jet Fighter-Bombers
26 *Martin Canberra B-57B* Bombers
6 *Martin Canberra RB-57* Bombers
15 *Sikorsky S-55 Hunters*
4 *Grumman HU-16A Albatross* Maritime Reconnaissance
12 *Lockheed F-104A Starfighters*
2 *Lockheed F-104B Starfighters*
6 *Lockheed C-130E Hercules* Transport
4 *Kaman HH-43B Huskie Hunters*
25 *Cessna T-37B* Jet Trainers

NAVY

7 Coastal Minesweepers

1 Tug
2 Oilers
4 "Battle" Class Destroyers
2 "CV" Class Destroyers
2 "Ch" Class Destroyers

Of these, the first three items were directly supplied by the United States. The rest were refitted under the Military Assistance Programme. The two "Ch" Class Destroyers were initially purchased by the United States for Pakistan. One Water Carrier, two Tugs and one Oiler were purchased from Italy under the Programme and transferred to Pakistan. One Submarine—"Trench" Class *PNS GHAZI* (now sunk)—was loaned to Pakistan. Recently an unspecified number of riverboats and coasters were supplied to Pakistan by USA.

In addition, all the air bases in Pakistan-Mauripur, Samungli, Drigh Road, Peshawar, Kohat, Risalpur, Lahore, Sargodha, Multan, Chaklala, Nawabshah, Gilgit, Chitral, Malir and Miranshah—were built up by NATO standards under the US Military Assistance Programme. Early-warning surveillance radars facing India were installed under this Programme at Badin, Multan, Sargodha and Peshawar. A microwave communication network was also developed under the CENTO base programme.

The US military assistance to Pakistan amounted to $730 million in supply of hardware and another $565 million in defence support assistance for the maintenance of the armed forces. Besides, the United States also undertook to train the personnel of the Pakistani armed forces.

CHINA

ARMY

Infantry and Artillery equipment for two divisions (*AK 47* rifles, light and medium machine-guns, 60 mm, 81 mm, 120 mm mortars, 100 mm field guns) and 225 *T-59* medium tanks.

AIR FORCE

1 Squadron of *11-28* Bombers
4 Squadrons of *MIG-19* Interceptors

NAVY

The Chinese are believed to have supplied Pakistan an unspecified number of riverboats and coasters since March 1971.

In addition the Chinese have assisted Pakistan in setting up the two major ordnance factories in Pakistan: one at Joydebpur, the other in Taxila.

Pakistan has recently revealed that all these supplies were free of cost.

UNITED KINGDOM

4 Patrol Boats

WEST GERMANY

90 *F-86 Sabre* Jets through Iran
Cobra Anti-Tank Missiles

FRANCE

5 *Alouette-III* Helicopters
24 *Mirage-III* Fighters
3 "Daphne" Class Submarines

IRAN

4 *Lokheed C-130E Hercules* Transport Planes

ITALY

8 *Midget* Submarines and 8 *Chariot* Two-Man Submarines

USSR

MI 8 Helicopters (number not known)
200 130 mm guns
150 *T-55* Tanks
Mobile Radar Sets
Spares for *MIG-19*

While the above transactions are by and large confirmed, the following transactions are not confirmed but are plausible:

100 *Patton* Tanks from West European sources

Another quantity of *Patton* Tanks from Iran-Turkey

More *F-86 Sabre* Jets from Saudi Arabia and Iran not exceeding 50.

Ammunition, aircraft Spares, communication and other equipment from the United States, Western Europe and China (quantities not ascertainable).

(*Courtesy:* K. Subrahmanyam, Director, Institute for Defence Studies and Analyses, New Delhi).

APPENDIX 'B'

Bangla Desh—Topographical

The new nation of Bangla Desh, most recently East Pakistan and East Bengal before that, is surrounded by five states of the Indian Union: West Bengal, Meghalaya, Assam, Tripura, and Mizoram—and, of course, the Bay of Bengal. The country itself is divided into four major administrative sectors—Khulna, Rajshahi, Dacca and Chittagong—each of which is, for administrative purposes, further sub-divided into various districts.

With the exception of low ranges in the Chittagong Hill Tract, a plateau north of Dacca and a few forest areas, Bangla Desh is comprised of a vast plain interspersed by the numerous tributaries of three major rivers; the Ganges (or Padma), the Brahamaputra and the Meghna. This plain, formed by the alluvial deposits of the three rivers, is fertile and favourable to agricultural pursuit. The alluvial soil, several hundred feet thick, is composed of silt, clay and an admixture of various types of fine sand.

The Sunderbans, as the tract of creeks, channels, swampy islands and jungles of the Ganges Delta nearest the sea is known, constitute a major feature of the area. These run inland to a distance varying between 60 and 80 miles and, with their numerous water-courses, enforce largely water-borne forms of transport on the local inhabitants.

The only topographical relief to the plain is provided by the three ranges in the Chittagong district, running roughly on a north-south axis, which reach an altitude of 1,200 feet above sea level, and the Madhupur forest area, the previously mentioned plateau north of Dacca, which varies in altitude from 40–100 feet.

Climatically Bangla Desh is a classic example of the humid tropics—perpetually warm and abundantly blessed with rain. The monsoon season, preceded by thunderstorms in March and April, continues from May until October. During this period the humidity is, perhaps, a trifle high for the comfort of those accustomed to more arid climes.

Cyclones, a perennial hazard for those living nearest the Bay of Bengal, occasionally reach epic ferocity and exact a high toll in life and property. Fortunately for the other inhabitants of Bangla Desh these cyclonic disturbances tend to dissipate as they travel inland and pose no serious threat to the northern districts.

The countryside, barring the less easily cultivated areas of the Sunderbans and Chittagong Hill Tract, gives an impression of verdant, lush, well-tilled prosperity. The groves of mangoes and bamboos, the well-manicured plantations and variety of palm trees re-inforce this pleasing impression.

Bangla Desh is perhaps historically best known for its jute crop—a staple which caused the foundation of the jute mills in Calcutta in pre-partition India. Rice, however, is another major crop—in some places grown with such phenomenal success that three harvests a year are possible. Apart from the principal crops, rice and jute, all types of vegetables, sugarcane, potatoes and oil seeds are grown in abundance.

The transportation and communications networks of Bangla Desh are affected to a more than usual extent by its topography. Inland water transport, clearly, plays a crucial role in the Sunderbans and is also heavily relied upon in other parts of the country for the movement of goods and produce to and from major market areas. Roads and railways, conforming to the estuarine features of the region run roughly parallel to each other, on north-south lines. East-west movement by other than riverine transport is difficult.

The waterways, with the exception of the Sunderbans area where they are omnipresent, are grouped around the rivers Surma Meghna, Jamuna (and its tributory, the Brahmaputra) and Padma. These rivers have the effect of quadrisecting the country into natural rather than administrative divisions. The Surma-Meghna waters, flowing southwest from the Sylhet sector, "cordons off" the eastern part of the country (Comila, Noakhali, Chittagong, Cox's Bazar). Between the Surma-Meghna and the Jamuna, which runs very nearly on a north-south axis, is Mymensingh, on the Brahmaputra. The Jamuna and the Padma border the northwestern region with its major cities—Rangpur, Dinajpur, Bogra and Rajshahi. The topography of the northwest is relatively less punctuated by rivers than the other three. The Padma, in its south-easterly course from Rajshahi, delineates the southern region; notably Kushtia, Jessore, Khulna and, in the Sunderbans, Chalna. Dacca's situation in the centre is nearly a confluence for all three rivers and their attendant economic traffic.

The alluvial, one might almost say aquatic, character of the geography of Bangla Desh has perhaps been covered in tedious detail but its relevance to the conduct of any military operation in that area is immense. While Bangla Desh might be a paradise for waterfowl it must be a nightmare for a campaign planner.

Under peacetime conditions with all bridges and approach roads intact the east-west movement of a large body of men and equipment would be difficult. In war, with the urgency of the time factor poised like the sword of Damocles over the Indian forces, it presented formidable obstacles. The Mukti Bahini, in its emergent formation as the Mukti Fouj, had quickly and correctly appreciated the importance of hampering the mobility of Pakistani troops. In that terrain, clearly, the ability to cross a river with relative ease is a necessary condition for rapid movement. Among the earliest dramatic successes of the Mukti Fouj were bridge sabotage and subsequent ambush of the stalled Pakistanis. Unfortunately, a dynamited bridge is impersonal and will delay enemy and ally alike. The "air-bridging" operations, cooperative efforts between the Army and IAF, were expediently adopted to over that particular hurdle.

This terrain, so obviously difficult for military manoeuvre is, particularly in the south, laced or webbed with small, unpredictable, criss-cross channels. Even after the monsoons have abated, and the larger rivers have shrunk from ocean-esque appearance to something more credibly riverine, numerous creeks and channels make of Bangla Desh a country of island stretches. An army and its attendant equipment fords a river with considerable effort; crossing a marsh (to arrive at yet another river) is not that much easier.